RUDOLF FRIML

AMERICAN

Composers

A list of books in the series
appears at the end of this volume.

Rudolf Friml

William Everett

UNIVERSITY OF
ILLINOIS PRESS
Urbana and Chicago

Library of Congress Cataloging-in-Publication Data
Everett, William A., 1962–
Rudolf Friml / William Everett.
p. cm. — (American composers)
Includes bibliographical references, discography, and index.
ISBN-10 0-252-03381-7 (cloth : alk. paper)
ISBN-13 978-0-252-03381-0 (cloth : alk. paper)
1. Friml, Rudolf, 1879–1972.
2. Composers—United States—Biography.
I. Title.
ML410.F94E84   2008
780.92—dc22 [B]   2008012690

To Lynda

CONTENTS

PREFACE

THIS BOOK, FOLLOWING THE TENETS OF the series in which it appears, is intended to provide a short, readable introduction to the life of Rudolf Friml and his music. It is not meant to be comprehensive but rather selective. I have attempted to provide enough information to give readers an idea of the extraordinary life of Friml, one that lasted just short of ninety-three years. The opening chapter surveys Friml's life from his boyhood in Prague through his activities as a pianist and a composer of piano music in America during the early twentieth century. Since he is most famous for his work on Broadway, I focus on that dimension of his output; four of the book's seven chapters are dedicated to Friml's contributions to the American musical theater. For many of the works mentioned in the text, the date and theatre of the premiere appear in parentheses after the title. Chapter 2 surveys his works before *Rose Marie;* chapters 3 and 4 center on his two most successful Broadway scores, *Rose Marie* and *The Vagabond King;* and chapter 5 addresses the shows that followed *The Vagabond King.* Chapter 6 concerns Friml's life away from Broadway and includes information on his film musicals, nontheatrical works, activities as a pianist, and private life. The final chapter addresses Friml's influence on the Broadway musical and concludes with remarks about his impressive legacy.

The largest repository of material concerning the life and work of Rudolf Friml is the Rudolf Friml Collection (collection 20) in the Music Library Special Collections at UCLA. The vast holdings include manuscripts, Ozalid reproductions, printed music, business and personal correspondence, newspaper and magazine clippings, photographs, posters, private and commercial recordings, unpublished reminiscences, and other materials. Friml donated three boxes of materials in 1971, while his widow, Kay, donated nearly fifty additional boxes in 2004. As of 2008, much of the collection remains unprocessed.

The UCLA materials are by no means the only ones related to Friml and his legacy. Unpublished librettos for shows on which Friml collaborated with Otto Harbach (most of which date from the second decade of the twentieth century and are discussed in chapter 2) are in the Otto Harbach Papers in the Billy Rose Theatre Collection at the New York Public Library for the Performing Arts. The papers also include correspondence and contracts related to the productions. Materials regarding Friml's work in Hollywood, including film stills and clipping files, were consulted at the Margaret Herrick Library of the Academy of Motion Picture Arts and Sciences. Unless otherwise noted, all primary sources consulted for this study come from the above-mentioned collections.

ACKNOWLEDGMENTS

PRODUCING A MUSICAL THEATER work is a collaborative effort; so is writing a book. Many people contributed to this book in different ways, and I am grateful to them all.

First and foremost I would like to thank Mrs. Kay Friml (1913–2007), not only for granting me access to her late husband's letters, manuscripts, and other materials but also for her inspiration in bringing this project to its completion. Likewise, Lewis Baker was invaluable in helping me sort through the Friml materials in Los Angeles and in securing permissions for this book.

Judith McCullough of the University of Illinois Press invited me to submit a proposal when the American Composers series was in its formative stage; I am extremely indebted to her for her unfaltering support of this project from inception through completion. I would also like to thank Laurie Matheson, acquisitions editor of the University of Illinois Press, for her help and advice regarding this book as it went through the production process, and to Julie Bush for careful copyediting. To the two anonymous reviewers: my heartfelt thanks for your keen observations and insightful comments. I greatly appreciate the time and effort you spent reading the manuscript and for your helpful suggestions that made this a better book. Thanks also to Sarah Jacobs and Melinda Lein for their close reading of the manuscript. I am also extremely appreciative to Sara Davis Buechner for her enthusiasm for Friml's music and for wonderful conversations and insights about the composer and his work, including the dialogue held on our restaurant trek in Los Angeles. Her two recordings (thus far) of Friml's music have been tremendous sources of inspiration. I would be remiss not to thank my colleagues at other universities who invited me to give guest lectures on Friml, including Paul Laird at the University of Kansas and Jane and George Ferencz at the University of Wisconsin, Whitewater. Many thanks for your gracious hospitality.

The majority of research for this book was funded by a research award from the University of Missouri Research Board. I am grateful to the board and to the anonymous reviewers of my proposal for this grant. I would also like to thank those at the University of Missouri–Kansas City's Miller Nichols Library: Chuck Haddix and the staff of the Marr Sound Archive for their help in locating recordings of Friml's music; the Interlibrary Loan Department for obtaining hard-to-find music; and Laura Gayle Green, music/media librarian, Debbie Keeton, and their student assistants for their help with various aspects of this project. I am deeply appreciative to my colleagues in the musicology area at UMKC, Olga Ackerly, Andrew Granade, and Sarah Tyrrell, and to the many wonderful students in my classes at the UMKC Conservatory of Music and Dance for their enthusiastic support of my work. I am especially indebted to Nicholas Philips for his interest in Friml's piano music, John Blair for his help with Friml's New York connections, and David Kováč for his interest in Friml's Czech connections and translations of various articles, book excerpts, and Web sites from Czech to English. I would also like to thank Jindřiška Kováčová for her help in locating materials in the Czech Republic and Randall Pembrook, former dean of the UMKC Conservatory of Music and Dance, for his support of my research.

To librarians at the Music Library Special Collections at the University of California, Los Angeles, especially Lauren Buisson, the British Library, the New York Public Library, the Library of Congress, the National Library of the Czech Republic, and the Prague Conservatory Archives, my heartfelt thanks. Michael Beckermann, Bunker Clark, Elizabeth Hille Cribbs, John Koegel, Michael Pisani, Katie Schuermann, and Ann Sears were extremely helpful in various phases of this project, and I owe each of them tremendous thanks.

Finally, thank yous go to my dear wife, Lynda, who endured endless hours of Friml tales and loads of time with me in front of the computer wearing "big ears" (stereo headphones) while listening to Friml's music and who accompanied me on trips to see productions of *Rose Marie* and *The Vagabond King*, and to Bentley, the leading canine authority on Rudolf Friml.

RUDOLF FRIML

I | From Prague
to America

IN MICHAEL CHABON'S Pulitzer Prize–winning novel, *The Amazing Adventures of Kavalier & Clay*, Joe Kavalier leaves his hometown of Prague and journeys to America, where he emerges as a significant figure in American popular culture.[1] Rudolf Friml (1879–1972), like his fictional counterpart, was a Prague native who left an indelible imprint on American life. Kavalier was Jewish and left Prague to escape Hitler, whereas Friml was Catholic and came to America as a burgeoning piano virtuoso. Kavalier became a famous comic book illustrator; Friml developed into a leading Broadway composer. For both young men, the journey from Prague continued—physically, spiritually, and creatively—after arriving in America.

Friml lived for nearly ninety-three years. He credited his longevity to the power of music. Even in his nineties, he still played piano four to six hours every day, once saying, "I'm so full of music that if I don't sit down and let some of it flow I think I would burst from the pressure."[2] Although Friml achieved his greatest fame and fortune on Broadway, he also wrote songs, solo piano works, and film music. Late in life, he turned toward orchestral music as his primary means of musical expression.

Friml's apex as a Broadway composer arrived during the first third of the twentieth century. He was a master of the late Romantic style and excelled in the world of the operetta. His greatest hits and the shows that made him a household name include *The Firefly* (1912), *Katinka* (1915), *Rose Marie* (1924), *The Vagabond King* (1925), and *The Three Musketeers* (1928). Songs such as "Sympathy," "Indian Love Call," "Song of the Vagabonds," and "Only a Rose" touched the hearts of millions. But during the 1930s, public tastes changed, and for a creator whose commercial success rested largely on public reception, Friml had to decide whether to alter his style to please the public or to become old-fashioned. True to himself, Friml chose the latter path and remained staunchly proud of his decision.

Rudolf Antonín Frymel was born on December 2, 1879, in his family's home at Vejovodova Street no. 445 (new no. 1) in Prague and was baptized on December 11, 1879, at St. Jiljí Catholic Church in Prague. He was the youngest of three children born to František and Marie Frymel. His eldest sister, Barbora, was born in 1874 and died in 1877, two years before Rudolf's birth. His other sister, Zdeňka, was born on May 7, 1877. Rudolf remained close to his sister, who spent her entire life in Czech lands.

Friml's own account of the beginning of his musical career reads like something from a folk legend.[3] His father, an accordion-playing baker, was supposed to buy wood for the fire but instead spent the money on a piano for his son. The

Friml's house in Prague. Courtesy of Kay Friml.

future composer's mother was livid but realized that her husband made the right decision when their son's musical talents became increasingly obvious. The boy could pick out tunes by ear almost immediately, and his parents quickly secured lessons for him with a local teacher. Young Rudolf was not the best student for this traditional-minded teacher, for rather than playing scales and arpeggios as instructed, he preferred to improvise on them, much to his instructor's chagrin. The teacher complained that Friml was peculiar and should do only what he was told and nothing more. Friml's mother sided with her son in this disagreement and found not just one new teacher for him, but three. She believed that one teacher could not know everything and that a variety of approaches and opinions would ultimately make her son a stronger musician.

One of Friml's teachers was the local church choirmaster. He took Friml as a student under the condition that the boy would play organ for the 6:00 A.M. daily masses. Friml's mother agreed, aware that her son knew the liturgy and its music by heart. Friml came from a strong Roman Catholic family and remained devoted to his faith throughout his life.

In his youth, Rudolf knew that he wanted to be a professional musician. He was concerned, however, that his surname was too long and needed to be abridged. He scribbled various contractions and variants of Frymel until he came up with the one that suited him: Friml.[4] Thus, Friml created his own family name.

In 1895, Friml entered the Prague Conservatory in the piano class, where he remained until 1901. His teachers included two of the most important pianists of the era: Josef Jiránek, a student of Bedřich Smetana, and Hanuš Trneček. Rosters for the piano classes during Friml's years at the conservatory are in the Prague Conservatory Archives. Friml's name appears on these lists as Friml, indicating that he was already using his new name when he began his conservatory training.

On the rosters for years two through five (1896–97 through 1899–1900), the letter *B* appears beside Friml's name in blue pencil. He is the only student to have this indication. The meaning of the letter is not known; wishful thinking would interpret it as an abbreviation for *Besten*, an indication of Friml's exalted place in his class. (German was the language of record for the conservatory at the time.) None of his classmates went on to establish names for themselves as important pianists; only Friml forged a career as a concert artist.

While at the conservatory, Friml also studied composition with Antonín Dvořák, who had returned to his teaching duties at the conservatory in 1895 after his American sojourn.[5] Unfortunately, student rosters for the composition classes have not survived, if they existed in the first place. Likewise, it is not known how long Friml studied with Dvořák or how formal the tutelage was.

Friml described Dvořák as a very busy person. Composition came first for Dvořák, according to Friml, who remembered his teacher as "a rather nervous man who would be thinking about something else when you talked to him."[6] Friml enjoyed walking with Dvořák and asking the composer questions about music and especially about orchestration. The aspiring composer learned a great deal on their walks, absorbing his teacher's words in an informal setting. He repeatedly stated Dvořák's main advice to him: "He told me to stick to my melodies. 'Take a theme and develop it. Don't jump around like a goat.'"[7] Friml adhered to this principal in his music, which is almost always melody-driven.

Friml never graduated from the conservatory, for he was expelled on May 1, 1901.[8] The orchestra at the National Theatre went on strike, and its faithful turned out in droves whenever it gave concerts independent of the National Theatre. The orchestra was planning a concert at the Rudolfinum, next door to the conservatory building, and invited Friml to play. At the time, the conservatory absolutely forbade its students to play in public before their formal conservatory-sponsored debuts, but Friml ignored the rules and joined the orchestra in its performance. Jiránek and other conservatory professors told Friml that he was making a big mistake as far as the school was concerned and that if he played the concert, he would be dismissed and not receive his diploma. Ignoring their warnings, Friml played the concert and was expelled, as promised. He recalled Jiránek's response backstage immediately after the performance: "But he was so proud of me[;] he fixed my suit, combed my hair and told me to go and take another bow. He said, 'You don't have to worry. Your diploma is in your fingers.'"[9]

Friml was never one to respond unquestioningly to authority. In his late teens, after his expulsion from the conservatory, he was described as one who "lived the life of a Bohemian—thoughtlessly."[10] He was Bohemian not only ethnically but also philosophically. Friml believed strongly in fairness and rights for individuals, evident here in his choice to play with an orchestra that was on strike. This same passion for social justice is obvious in his stirring music for songs such as "The Mounties," "Song of the Vagabonds," and "March of the Musketeers," all of which have lyrics concerning justice defeating oppression.

All was not lost for Friml in 1901, however, for he found employment as a rehearsal pianist for the ballet at the National Theatre. As the Czech ballet director Augustin Berger recalled, Friml's mother approached him and begged him to hire her son. Berger went to the director of the ballet, F. A. Šubrt, and inquired about the possibility of employing Friml, who already had a reputation as a fine pianist. Šubrt was reluctant, fearing repercussions from the conservatory for appointing someone it had expelled. Berger ultimately decided to engage the young pianist, and when Friml arrived at rehearsal the next day, the director described him as "a long haired, sun tanned sympathetic young man."[11] He called Friml "an excellent and also an amusing and happy-go-lucky korepetitor [accompanist]."[12] Friml had begun to make his mark on the musical world.

Early Compositions

Among Friml's earliest published compositions are songs with Czech texts. His opus 1, *Písně Závišovy* (Songs of Záviš), a song cycle to poems by Jan Červenka, was first published in 1901 and remains popular in Czech lands in the early twenty-first century. The five songs in the cycle—"Jen trochu lásky" (Just a Little Bit of Love), "Pro Vás!" (For You), "Což je to hřích?" (So Is It a Sin?), "Zda si někdy vzpomínáte?" (Do You Ever Remember?), and "Za tichých nocí" (Through Quiet Nights)—are historical mainstays of the Czech song repertory. Záviš, the namesake of the cycle, is an ancient Czech hero, and the cycle fits nicely into the idealization of the past that was a significant part of emerging Czech identity. Friml evokes a late Romantic musical style reminiscent of Smetana, with lyrical vocal lines, rhapsodic piano parts, and a chromatically extended tonal vocabulary.

The cycle's extraordinary publication legacy offers further proof of its tremendous popularity. Between 1901 and 1905, the Czech publisher F. A. Urbánek issued three editions of the set, and by 1946, the original version for high voice and piano had been published thirteen times.[13] Adaptations soon appeared for middle voice, solo piano, violin and piano, solo accordion, and male chorus (arranged by František Špilka).

Soprano Emma Destinn (1878–1930) had the cycle translated into German and included it in her concerts. She arranged to have the songs published in Germany and gave Friml the royalties, which he used to help finance his first trip to America.[14] Destinn's father was a friend of Friml's, and he introduced the aspiring composer to his daughter, who was then on the roster of the Berlin Opera House. She became a great supporter of the young Bohemian and even asked him to go to Berlin and write an opera for her. But Friml remained in Prague because of what he called "some infatuation."[15] The truth of the matter, according to Friml, was that Destinn was in love with him. She wrote him love letters that, when he shared them with his sister, made her cry. After Friml immigrated to America, he began writing love letters to Destinn. However, her replies were cold: "Now you write me love letters when the ocean is between us." Years later, when Destinn sang at the Metropolitan Opera in New York, she never invited Friml to any of her well-known parties.[16] She achieved tremendous fame in New

York, and although Friml never wrote an opera for her, Giacomo Puccini did; *La fanciulla del West* (The Girl of the Golden West, 1910) was written for her and tenor Enrico Caruso.

The final song of *Písně Závišovy* took on another dimension during the German occupation in the early 1940s. In 1941, it formed the centerpiece both musically and dramatically of the film *Za tichých nocí*, which shares its title with the song. The story is that of the song's composer, Záviš Herold (whose first name comes from the name of the song cycle), and his unhappy love. Although the film opens with a disclaimer that it is not based on any real person, the protagonist has a great deal in common with Friml, including his immigration to America.[17]

Friml wrote several more song cycles, all to Czech texts. Among these were *Nové písně Závišovy* (New Songs of Záviš), op. 14 (1905, texts by Jan Červenka), and *Na struně lásky* (On the String of Love), op. 19 (1909, texts by Karl Hašler). Like the first set of Záviš songs, these cycles are filled with flowing melodies and late Romantic harmonies.

In addition to songs, Friml also worked with larger mediums. His ballet "Slavnost Chrysanthem" (Festival of the Chrysanthemums) was added to the last act of a production of Sidney Jones's operetta *The Geisha* that opened at the National Theatre in Prague on May 11, 1900.[18] Friml was still a student at the conservatory at the time, and the composition predates his employment at the National Theatre. Friml was therefore no stranger to Berger when the future ballet accompanist's mother approached the director the next year about hiring her son. The score demonstrates tremendous originality on Friml's part. Numerous trademark Orientalist features appear, including prominent uses of staccato, dotted rhythms, pizzicato, and grace notes. All of these features contributed to an exotic sound when compared with that of mainstream European orchestral music of the time. Friml, who also orchestrated the work, included orchestral bells, snare drum, and cymbals as part of his attempt to create an Oriental sound world.

At Berger's request, Friml extended the ballet into a full act.[19] Berger directed productions of the expanded work in 1905 at both the National Theatre in Prague (as *Den v Japonsku* [A Day in Japan]) and the Dresden Opera House (as *Auf Japan* [From Japan]).[20]

Another composition that solidified Friml's early reputation in Prague was *Indiánská píseň* (Indian Song). The solo piano work was published in 1905 in Prague by Mojmír Urbánek and became instantly popular.[21] It also appeared in versions for violin and piano and for orchestra. František Ondříček, the highly esteemed Czech violinist who actively promoted Dvořák's Violin Concerto, played it in a recital in Prague on November 12, 1905, and the Czech Philharmonic played the orchestral version at two concerts held in the hall of the City Market on November 26 and December 7, 1905.[22] Audiences raved at the orchestral performances; their fifteen minutes of applause resulted in the work being repeated twice.[23]

"Indian Song," a different work altogether than Rose Marie's "Indian Love Call," brought a waft of exoticism to Prague.[24] Its title is reminiscent of the second movement of Dvořák's Violin Sonata, "Indian Lament." The evocative work consists of a large introduction in G minor and a main section in G major. Recognizable Indianist identifiers appear throughout, including repeated bass notes, the Phrygian mode with its lowered second scale degree, drone fifths with grace notes, and a pentatonic melody. But the most pronounced Indianist motifs appear near the work's midpoint, when alternating thirds (G-E) marked with accents in the left hand precede minor seconds (E-flat-D) pounded in octaves. Friml adds words at this point: "hu-wa. hu-wa" for the thirds and "wara wara" for the semitones. These syllables, whether or not actually uttered in performance, nonetheless add a programmatic-based exoticism to the work.

The Pianist

At the beginning of the twentieth century, Friml wanted to be a virtuoso pianist in the grand tradition of Frédéric Chopin and Franz Liszt, both of whom, like Friml, were Slavs. Playing for the ballet at the National Theatre was not enough.

Friml's early international fame as a pianist came through his association with violinist Jan Kubelík (1880–1940), one of his classmates at the Prague Conservatory. Kubelík, a student of pedagogue Otakar Ševčik (author of the famous violin method), had an impressive musical career. Acclaimed as a "second Paganini," his forty-year concert life included tours to the United States, South America, East Asia, Australia, and Africa. Kubelík was known for his clean and agile technical precision, although his interpretations were sometimes regarded as backward-looking.[25]

Friml and Kubelík began their collaboration while students and, in order to earn money (since both came from poor families), toured Czech lands. They also traveled abroad in 1901 and gave performances in Germany and London prior to a six-concert tour of Russia. After hearing their London performance, American impresario Daniel Frohman engaged the violinist and pianist for a U.S. tour that ultimately included seventy-eight concerts between November 20, 1901, and March 24, 1902.[26] The tour constituted a milestone in the careers of both men.

Friml recalled one concert on the tour when the person in charge of the music forgot the piano parts. Kubelík panicked, as would be expected, but Friml, showing extreme self-confidence and self-control, told him not to worry, for he had it all memorized. Afterward, Kubelík told Friml that the pianist had never played better. From then on, according to Friml himself, he played everything from memory.[27]

Kubelík benefited more immediately from the tour than did Friml, for it catapulted the violinist to fame. Store window displays "a la Kubelík" featured hats, boots, scarves, and other items of the type Kubelík wore, and society women inundated him with marriage proposals. This was the beginning of an extremely lucrative time for Kubelík, who earned over half a million dollars in a single decade.[28]

Although the tour did not make Friml a star, it was significant, for it gave him added determination to embark on a solo performing career. A portrait painted in Prague in the early years of the century by Friml's friend Vladimir Šamberk captures the Czech pianist's dreams of glory. The long hair, striking features, and sophisticated dress all endorse the celebrity image.

Friml returned to the United States for tours in 1904 and again in 1906, when he settled in New York. His recitals included sonatas, character pieces, and

Portrait of Rudolf Friml by Vladimir Šamberk. Courtesy of Kay Friml.

improvisations. His program for the Briarcliff School in Briarcliff Manor, New York, on April 19, 1904, was as follows:

Sonata, op. 27, no. 2   Ludwig van Beethoven
Prelude, op. 3   Sergei Rachmaninoff
Polka in F major   Bedřich Smetana
Am Meeresufer   Smetana

Impromptu in F sharp minor, op. 36   Frédéric Chopin
Etude in F minor, op. 25, no. 2   Chopin
Nocturne, op. 15, no. 2[29]   Chopin
"Improvisation" (Extempore)   Friml

Caprice Espagnole   Moritz Moszkowski
Etude de concert, op. 4   Friml
Polonaise in A flat, op. 53   Chopin
Tannhäuser Ouverture   Richard Wagner–Franz Liszt[30]

He played a similar, though shorter, offering for an afternoon recital at New York's Mendelssohn Hall on December 7, 1904:

Sonata, op. 27[31]   Beethoven
Prelude, op. 5   Rachmaninoff
From the Old Time (improvisation)   Friml
La Chasse   Felix Mendelssohn
Impromptu in F sharp minor, op. 36   Chopin
Etude in C major, op. 10   Chopin
Nocturne, op. 15   Chopin
Menuetto, from the suite, op. 27   Josef Suk
Improvisation   Friml
Tannhäuser Ouverture   Wagner-Liszt[32]

Friml chose ambitious repertory. With the exception of the Beethoven sonata and one of Mendelssohn's *Songs without Words* ("La Chasse," op. 19, no. 3), all of the music on these representative concerts had some sort of Slavic connection, whether Russian (Rachmaninoff), Czech (Smetana, Suk, Friml), Polish (Moszkowski, Chopin), or Hungarian (Wagner-Liszt). By including his own music on the same program as that of famous Slavic piano virtuosos, Friml was asserting and defining his place among them.

Improvisation was a key component of every Friml recital, from the early years of the twentieth century through the early 1970s, when the nonagenarian pianist was still concertizing. He would improvise on either his own themes or those offered to him by the audience. The high level and originality of his improvisations consistently captured the attention of the critics.

On November 17, 1904, Friml made his Carnegie Hall debut playing his own Piano Concerto with the New York Symphony under the direction of Walter Damrosch. Friml had enormous respect for Damrosch, calling him "the greatest conductor of the American Orchestra."[33] The concerto is in one continuous movement with multiple sections (Maestoso—Adagio—Quasi Adagio—Quasi Berceuse—Allegro furioso).[34] As such, it follows the model of Liszt's Piano Concerto no. 1 in E flat (1832, rev. 1849, 1853, 1856) and predates Sergey Prokofiev's First Piano Concerto (1912).

Friml wrote out the orchestral score, but it was essentially illegible for both Damrosch and the orchestra. According to the composer, a professional copyist had to work through the night after the first rehearsal in order to create a legible score and set of parts. The solo part was presumably added to the score at a later date, for it is in different ink. Long solo passages are indicated by blank measures; in these instances, the piano part reappears just before the orchestra enters. Friml liked to tell the tale, which may be apocryphal, that he improvised a different cadenza at each rehearsal, and that this caused Damrosch tremendous consternation, for the conductor did not know when to bring in the orchestra. Friml finally settled on at least an ending for the cadenza, which is what is likely indicated in the score.

The reviewer for the *Musical Courier* was generally optimistic about the new concerto, calling it "an exceedingly ambitious work. It may want cohesiveness, continuity of thought, and it doubtless betrays certain incongruities and crudities; and it may not disclose a profound contrapuntal knowledge, but it certainly is replete with melody and is not devoid of felicitous harmonic devices. It keeps the pianist incessantly busy, and he has to overcome some very difficult feats. Friml performed his own work 'con amore,' and his playing was as joyous as it was brilliant."[35] An unnamed critic for the *New York Times* was less enthusiastic, describing the work as "a thing of shreds and patches, of short phrases dressed up in passages, [a] work of a highly 'pianistic' but otherwise insignificant character."[36]

The audience loved Friml and the new concerto, for they demanded five curtain calls after its performance. They were likewise enthusiastic about the solo pieces on the program as well as the improvisation on a theme given to Friml by an audience member. As the correspondent for the *Musical Courier* wrote, "[T]he audience came to hear the young Bohemian pianist and centred attention upon him. He appeared in the threefold capacity of composer, pianist and improviser, and it was difficult to determine in what particular field his talents best manifested themselves."[37] The only disappointing part of the concert, according to the same critic, was Friml's performance of the Grieg Piano Concerto, which he described as "too finical," or fastidious.

Solo Piano Music

In addition to his performing activities, Friml was also an extremely prolific composer for the piano. His more than one hundred solo piano works consist entirely of character pieces, published either as independent works or in suites and collections. (See the Selected Works section for a partial list of Friml's solo piano music.) The shadows of Friml's idols Chopin and Liszt loom large, and the miniatures are often tinged with hints of Smetana and Impressionism. Many individual pieces are waltzes, including some with female names such as "Valse Blanche" or "Valse Lucille," and others have descriptive qualifiers along the lines of "Valse Coquette," "Valse Poétique," and "Valse Triste." Other generic types also appear, including nocturnes, mazurka, etudes, and intermezzos. Many of Friml's solo piano pieces possess programmatic titles, such as "Egyptian Dance," "Night in Spain," and "La danse de demoiselles." The suites bear descriptive names such as *California Suite, Pastoral Scenes, A Day in May, After Sundown,* and *Russian Suite*. Each suite contains four to six movements, all of which have programmatic titles.

Friml, as a native of Prague, as a student of Dvořák's, and with a direct line of descent from Smetana, possessed a strong sense of Czech musical nationalism. He was extremely proud of his ethnic heritage, and this dimension is strongly evident in his solo piano music. His "Dumka" continues the tradition popularized by Dvořák of creating multisectional pieces, often in the style of laments. He also followed his teacher's example by creating a distinctively sentimental "Humoresque." Friml paid further homage to his ethnic heritage in the nationalistically titled "From Bohemian Woods" and "Bohemian Dance: Polka" and in the evocative "Bygone Days: Ach neni tu neni [Oh No, It's Not Here]—A Paraphrase on a Bohemian Folk-Song."

Music for solo piano appeared throughout Friml's long and illustrious career. After his Broadway debut with *The Firefly* in 1912, he continued to write extensively for solo piano. The publisher Gustave Schirmer took an interest in Friml's solo piano music and not only published it but also produced a fifty-nine-page catalog with commentary in 1914. Works are listed according to their level of difficulty. Comments are short, complimentary, and written as advice for the studio teacher. Schirmer's goal was to promote Friml and his music to piano teachers across the United States, stating in the preface: "Friml's works are famous for the fertile and spontaneous invention they display, and the fluent and unaffected style crowning their excellent workmanship and perfect mine of melody. They are generally accepted by educators as being ideal for teaching the average American student. The themes, while almost frankly appealing to the higher popular taste, carefully avoid the modern extravagances into which many present day writers fall, and never forsake an element of refined distinctiveness which lifts them far above the level of the ordinary."[38] What more could a teacher ask for? Here was quality music with popular appeal that young students might actually even practice for their lessons. A typical entry is that for "Valse Lucille," op. 85, no. 1: "The composer is well-known for the fine waltz melodies in his operas. The piece under consideration is in his best vein and can be used for social recreation or as a purely musical number. The melodies are charming, the rhythm piquant, and full of little surprises, giving it a distinctly unconventional quality. It will please the music lover, trained or untrained. Technically it belongs in the fourth year."[39]

Although such publicity would certainly seem to help the popularity of Friml and his music, its long-term effect was actually negative, for Friml's piano music became almost exclusively associated with teaching pieces, and its possibilities for concert performance faded. "Nice pieces for students" became an all-too-common description.

Fortunately, this reputation is changing. In large part due to Sara Davis Buechner's recording *Rudolf Friml Piano Works*, these engaging miniatures are being reevaluated as gems from the early-twentieth-century world of intimate and immediately pleasing piano music. Anthony Tommasini, in his *New York Times* review of the recording, called Friml's solo piano music "charming and surprisingly sophisticated" and described the music as "something very fine."[40]

Following typical practice of the time, many of these piano pieces also appeared in versions for various instrumental combinations; among the most common was violin and piano. Friml himself transcribed several of his solo piano works for Kubelík and him to play on their concerts, including "Bygone Days: Ach neni tu neni—A Paraphrase on a Bohemian Folk-Song." The piece endorses the late Romantic style of Friml's instrumental idiom through its evocative piano writing and rhapsodic violin part.

Friml's solo piano pieces exhibit a freshness and originality that stem from the composer's activity as a concert pianist. He knew what audiences wanted and wrote accordingly. His improvisational skills are likewise evident, for the melodies are natural and spontaneous, never belabored. Finally, Friml, in his solo piano music, explored a wide range of idioms, some lyrical, some sentimental, some humorous, some Bohemian, and some truly virtuosic. This accomplished stylistic versatility proved essential to Friml in 1912, when he began to write for Broadway, creating works in which different characters and dramatic situations were defined and endorsed by individual and distinctive types of music.

2 | The Emergence of a Broadway Composer

RUDOLF FRIML'S GREATEST fame comes from his work for the Broadway musical stage, for it was here, on the "Great White Way," that the composer achieved his crowning career successes. He was most prolific during the second decade of the twentieth century, during which time he wrote nine complete scores. He wrote fewer shows in the 1920s, but the quality and longevity of the works were greater. Friml's scores are typical of those of his contemporaries in that they include a variety of musical styles ranging from the nearly operatic to the vintage vaudevillian, but they are also different because of the sophistication of many of the songs and the ways in which various musical styles are used to amplify the plot. Although the stories that Friml set to music were not as developed as in midcentury "Golden Age" works such as those by Richard Rodgers and Oscar Hammerstein and their contemporaries, the integration of music, character type, and dramatic narrative in Friml's output serves as an important precedent for these later shows.

Three fundamental approaches existed within the realm of the Broadway musical during the early decades of the century: revue, musical comedy, and operetta. These were by no means mutually exclusive categories; in fact, it was the ingenious ways in which these genres could and would be cross-fertilized that distinguish many exemplary works of the time.

Revues themselves emerged out of several traditions, including minstrelsy and vaudeville. These staged spectacles consisted of skits and musical numbers in a format that sometimes followed a discernible plot, or at least a unifying topic. The stars and their songs were the focus of the musical side of the productions, while costumes, sets, and the trademark line of beautiful chorus girls provided visual spectacle. Revues were deeply rooted in their present, and many of the songs and skits included references to current events, media, political figures, and various aspects of popular culture. The most famous revues appeared in annual series, or "editions," as they were called. These included Florenz Zieg-feld's *Follies*, brothers J. J. and Lee Shubert's *The Passing Show* and *Artists and Models*, George White's *Scandals*, and Irving Berlin's *Music Box Revues*. Revues also appeared independent of series, such as the Shuberts' *Over the Top* (1917) with its World War I theme, dancing and singing stars Fred and Adele Astaire, and score by Sigmund Romberg. Legendary performers such as Fanny Brice, Will Rogers, Al Jolson, and W. C. Fields established their reputations in the genre, while composers such as Irving Berlin, George Gershwin, Irving Caeser, and Romberg wrote extensively for it.

Musical comedies were similar in style to revues but had linear dramatic plots. Because of their similarities, many composers, performers, and producers worked in both genres. Stories were typically set in the present day, often in New York City or its environs. They featured ordinary people who found themselves in somewhat realistic, though comic, situations. Gershwin, Jerome Kern, and the team of Richard Rodgers and Lorenz Hart were among the leading creators of musical comedy during the time of Friml's Broadway career.

Music for revues and musical comedies was most often in a popular style. Being "modern" genres that showcased the present, the shows endorsed the latest musical trends coming from Tin Pan Alley, ragtime, and social dance. Tin Pan Alley, a term referring to the American popular sheet music industry from the late nineteenth century through World War II, enjoyed a symbiotic relationship with Broadway—publishers marketed songs as being from Broadway productions, while Broadway composers had their work disseminated and popularized through publication. Tin Pan Alley songs are typically in verse-refrain form, where an often speech-like verse precedes a distinctly memorable melody, the refrain.

Ragtime, which was both a musical and a social phenomenon, had its roots in various African American musical discourses.[1] It achieved early popularity through solo piano pieces such as Scott Joplin's "Maple Leaf Rag" (1899) and "The Entertainer" (1902). Though Broadway composers did not employ strict ragtime form, they did embrace its characteristic syncopated melody against a non-syncopated bass along with its dotted rhythms. Socially, many saw ragtime as a threat to their moral values and heard the music as "unnatural," "mad," and even "evil." Others found it to be fresh, stimulating, and distinctively reflective of America and the emerging twentieth century.[2]

Ragtime opened new doors for popular dance.[3] Dances with animal names such as the turkey trot, the bullfrog hop, and the bunny hug, along with a dance developed by Harry Fox known as "Fox's trot" and subsequently "foxtrot," became increasingly popular. Dance sequences in revues and musical comedies often featured these steps, the same ones that audience members themselves danced. Thanks to ragtime, a conduit opened between the theater, the dance floor, and the studio.[4] In the world of dance instruction, the team of Vernon and Irene Castle standardized many ragtime steps and taught them to white sophisticates who were eager to learn them. The Castles are said to have tamed the rag, dancing and teaching it with grace and elegance.[5]

The third principal Broadway musical genre of the time was operetta. These conceptually escapist works were rooted in a Central European world and flaunted lavish musical scores filled with waltzes, marches, and various ethnic dances such as Hungarian czardas or Polish mazurka. Unlike in revue and musical comedy, where performers were the focus, in operetta, the musical scores reigned supreme. Singing styles were fundamentally operatic, and the overall approach was intensely romantic, with true love overcoming whatever challenges might have occurred so that the leads were together at the final curtain.

Central to the overall aesthetic of operetta was the idea of "Ruritania," an imaginary locale whose name comes from the setting for Anthony Hope's novel *The Prisoner of Zenda* (1894). Ruritania soon became synonymous with lands of dimwitted royals, colorfully dressed peasants, and extravagant foreigners (often from the Orient, either the Arab world or sometimes East Asia), all of whom lived blissfully oblivious to the real world in some sort of suspended nineteenth century. Most Ruritanian settings implied the Balkans, but wherever the Ruritanian clime, it was replete with castles and palaces.[6] Among the most famous Ruritanian operettas to play on Broadway was Franz Lehár's *The Merry Widow* (1907), an English-language adaptation of the Viennese original, *Die lustige Witwe* (1905).

Friml began his Broadway career in this multifaceted field of revue, musical comedy, and operetta. His work traversed orthodox generic conventions, and he drew materials from each approach to fit particular dramatic needs. Friml's experience writing character pieces for piano, through which he explored different musical idioms, provided him with solid training for creating variety among his songs for the musical stage, including those for the show with which he made his Broadway debut, *The Firefly*.

The Firefly

Prima donnas have reputations of being notoriously temperamental, and the diminutive Italian soprano Emma Trentini (1885–1959) was no exception. Victor Herbert (1859–1924), the esteemed leader of American operetta in the first decade of the twentieth century, wrote *Naughty Marietta* (1910) expressly for her. In 1912, the composer was conducting a performance of the operetta with Trentini in the title role when he famously stormed off the podium. Trentini was demanding an encore of "Italian Street Song" while Herbert wanted to continue with the performance. Neither would succumb to the other, and Herbert left the pit, vehemently vowing never again to work with the prima donna. This would not have necessarily been a huge problem, except that Herbert had already agreed to write another operetta for the spirited soprano, a work that was to be called *The Firefly*.

The new show's producer, Arthur Hammerstein (1872–1955, son of impresario Oscar [1847–1919] and uncle of famed lyricist and librettist Oscar 2nd [1895–1960]), found himself in dire need of a composer. Max Dreyfus, head of Harms Music, suggested that he take a chance on the young Friml, whose reputation at the time was that of an aspiring pianist and a composer of attractive piano miniatures.[7] Dreyfus was a very powerful figure in the music world, and his opinions were held in high regard. Hammerstein, who had heard Friml's ballet music in Dresden, took Dreyfus's advice and hired Friml to write the score.[8] This choice carried a significant risk for Hammerstein, for Friml's only direct experience working in the theater was as a rehearsal pianist for the ballet in Prague. His music had never appeared on a Broadway stage, and here he was replacing the great Victor Herbert! Not only that, but on his first Broadway outing, he would be writing a showpiece for one of the era's finest luminaries, Emma Trentini. Hammerstein made the right decision, for *The Firefly* was a critical and commercial success and paved the way for Friml's American career and legacy.

Otto Harbach (1873–1963), then working as Otto Hauerbach, was the show's librettist and lyricist. The talented Salt Lake City–born wordsmith began his professional career as an English professor at Whiman College in Walla Walla, Washington, before moving to New York, where he began working on his Ph.D. at Columbia University. Deciding that teaching was not for him, he worked as a journalist before collaborating with composer Karl Hoschna on the Broadway musical *The Three Twins* in 1908. He and Hoschna wrote four more shows before the composer's death in 1911. Harbach found himself in need of a new composer-collaborator, and Friml needed an experienced librettist. Hammerstein brought the two men together and, with his role as producer, created the triune partnership of Hammerstein, Harbach, and Friml. Including *The Firefly*, the trio worked together on eleven shows.

In the Cinderella-esque story, Nina Corelli, an Italian street singer in New York City, escapes an oppressive guardian by disguising herself as a cabin boy, Antonio, on Mrs. van Dare's Bermuda-bound yacht. Before departure, Geraldine, Mrs. van Dare's daughter, sees her fiancé, Jack Travers, talking to Nina and seethes with jealousy. On board, everyone adores "Tony," except for Geraldine, who says he reminds her of a street singer. Professor Franz lavishes special attention on the disguised singer, for he thinks he has found a wonderful choirboy with great promise for a professional career and tutors him (her) on proper vocal technique. By the final curtain, the jilted Geraldine has found a husband, and Nina, no longer cross-dressed, is both a renowned opera singer and Jack's wife.

Emma Trentini in act 2 of The Firefly. *Billy Rose Theatre Division, The New York Library for the Performing Arts, Astor, Lenox and Tilden Foundations.*

Since *The Firefly* was a vehicle for Emma Trentini, her music dominates the score. Friml's songs allowed the soprano to display her vocal virtuosity, and his styles ranged from Italian street songs and musical comedy numbers to lyrical ballads and opera arias. The various musical idioms are not employed haphazardly but rather accentuate character-driven dimensions of the female lead. Nina's professional development from a street singer to an opera star is chronicled through her evolving music. Her first song is the Neapolitan-sounding "Giannina Mia," which is even marked "Italian Street Song" in the score, providing a direct link to Victor Herbert's "Italian Street Song," an encore of which instigated the series of events that resulted in Friml writing *The Firefly*. Nina's early vocal training is apparent in the light and virtuosic "Love Is Like a Firefly," during which the singer must demonstrate her abilities to alternate immediately between staccato and lyrical passages. Her arrival as a major opera star is apparent in the final act when she sings the decidedly operatic "Kiss Me and 'Tis Day." This approach to character development through music is rare in shows from this decade and foreshadows Jerome Kern's musical treatment of Magnolia in *Show Boat* (1927) and Frederick Loewe's of Guenevere in *Camelot* (1960).

During act 2, when Trentini disguises herself as a boy, the prima donna's (or *primo uomo's*?) music is much more in the style of musical comedy, with its characteristic syncopation and dotted rhythms. Her three songs in the act not only root the show in its present day but also provide additional opportunities for Trentini to display her vocal versatility. "Tommy Atkins" is in the style of a military march, and Trentini performed the number in military uniform, much to the audience's delight. Tommy Atkins was a nickname for British soldiers that was widely used during the nineteenth century and would have been familiar to those sailing to the British colony of Bermuda in 1912. In the jocular "We're Going to Make a Man of You," Jack and his friends want to help Tony achieve manhood, a plan doomed to fail, although none of them realizes this. Finally, Nina sings the charmingly lyrical "When a Maid Comes Knocking at Your Heart" to Jack in order to educate him on appropriate responses to female advances. He refuses to listen to her as a woman, so she must dress as a man in order to offer him sage advice.

One of the show's most celebrated songs was the waltz "Sympathy," sung by the secondary male lead John Thurston to a heartbroken Geraldine van Dare. The waltz and its evocations of love worked for the sympathizer, for he ends up marrying Geraldine. This particular waltz is characteristic of a "hesitation waltz," in which dramatic pauses—or hesitations—interrupt the graceful musical flow.

The Firefly's performance history was solid, though not remarkable. It opened at the Lyric Theatre on December 2, 1912, and played for a respectable 120 performances before touring throughout America.[9] The show did not fare well abroad, however; the most significant international production was in Sydney, Australia (April 30, 1921, Her Majesty's Theatre). The 1937 film version had an entirely different story and only a bit of the original music. Starring Jeanette MacDonald and Allan Jones, "The Firefly" was now a Spanish spy (MacDonald) working to save her country from Napoleon. (See chapter 6 for further information on the film.)

On the Wings of *The Firefly: High Jinks* and *Katinka*

The Firefly immediately established Friml as a significant Broadway figure. He did not have to do hack work, writing a song here and there hoping to get something added into someone else's show, as was the norm for a neophyte composer. Rather, Friml's first Broadway credit was a complete show, and a good one at that. Friml ably rode this wave of success for the next decade, until *Rose Marie* catapulted him to even greater fame and glory. His collaboration with Arthur Hammerstein and Otto Harbach on *The Firefly* laid the foundation for a series of works that included elements of operetta within a fundamentally musical comedy context. Some works leaned toward operetta, foreshadowing *Rose Marie*, but most were happily at home in the realm of farcical musical comedy.

One of the plot devices in *The Firefly* concerns star-crossed lovers, a centuries-old dramatic scheme. (Consider Shakespeare's plays, which are filled with such romances, where various impersonations, cross-dressings, mistaken identities, and comic mishaps all get resolved before the final curtain.) Many of Friml's shows after *The Firefly* are farces, comic works in which authority, order, and morality are put at risk and ordinary people find themselves in extraordinary situations. Music for such plays needed to fit their overall light-spirited character and were often fast-paced and unsentimental. Being "modern" works, the scores frequently included "modern" syncopated numbers of the type that Friml had written for act 2 of *The Firefly*.

The second and third Friml-Harbach-Hammerstein collaborations, *High Jinks* (December 10, 1913, Lyric Theatre) and *Katinka* (December 22, 1915, 44th Street Theatre), built upon the success of *The Firefly*, the former leaning more toward musical comedy and the latter toward operetta. *High Jinks* was a "musical farce," according to its title page, while *Katinka* followed many of the tenets of Continental practice. Both shows demonstrated an integrated approach to music and story, and characters were distinguished and defined through their music. They also surpassed *The Firefly* in the lengths of their runs: whereas *The*

Firefly had a solid 120 Broadway performances, *High Jinks* played 213 times and *Katinka* 220.

Central to the plot of *High Jinks* is a magic elixir of the same name that, while intended to cure a multitude of ailments, causes whoever inhales it to laugh and fall in love.[10] The musical is set in France, act 1 in the flower garden of the private sanitarium of Gaston Thorne, a fashionable Parisian neurologist, and acts 2 and 3 at the Hotel DePavillion, a bathing resort on the French coast. The colorful comic characters of the cast, all of whom succumb to the power of High Jinks, come to France because of Dr. Thorne, who never refuses the embraces of his female patients as gratitude for his medical services. Among Thorne's visitors are Dick Wayne, an American explorer who discovered High Jinks in Tibet and has brought some to the neurologist, and Sylvia Dale, a Folies Bergère singer who becomes Dick's love interest. Thorne had previously operated on Sylvia's vocal chords, and she has returned for a check-up. The obese American lumber magnate Jim Jeffreys has come to Thorne for weight-loss treatment, not knowing that he will encounter his wife who had left him twenty-three years earlier, the world-weary Adelaide. Monsieur Jacques Rabelais is irate at Thorne for accepting a kiss from his wife, and Chi-Chi, the show's ingenue, poses as the romantic interest (or wife) of Jim, Dick, and Thorne. Comic mishaps fill the three acts, and the show ends with Dick waving a perfume-laced handkerchief that causes the entire cast to smile, forget their romantic mishaps, and enjoy being in love.

Friml's score for *High Jinks* is in a substantially lighter vein than that of *The Firefly*, befitting the new show's comic nature. The two most prominent numbers in *High Jinks* are "Something Seems Tingle-Ingleing" and "Love's Own Kiss."[11] Both songs appear early in act 1 and are reprised several times as musical signifiers for the farce's two interrelated dramatic ideas: the perfume's effects and falling in love. The two songs are in noticeably different styles: the first is a catchy musical comedy number; the second is an operetta waltz. Friml thus utilizes distinctive musical idioms to amplify plot elements, whether it is the carefree joy of inhaling High Jinks or the emotional sentiment of falling in love.

Dick introduces the enticing properties of High Jinks in "Something Seems Tingle-Ingleing," a comic number with an effusive refrain characterized by gently cascading dotted rhythms. The song returns in the finale of act 2 and again in that of act 3, where it forms the basis for the denouement as everyone's romantic confusions are blamed on the inhalant. (This recalls the end of Johann Strauss II's *Die Fledermaus*, when champagne is held responsible as the impetus for the evening's escapades.)

By contrast, "Love's Own Kiss" is a grand waltz. Sylvia and Dick introduce it early in the show, and the song returns in the course of the act 1 and act 2 finales. One phrase in the lyric anticipates *Rose Marie*'s "Indian Love Call" from just over a decade later: "While your voice seems calling me, calling, enthralling me" prefigures the more famous "When I'm calling you." In choosing a waltz as the primary love duet, Friml continued the European operetta trope of equating true love with waltzes. (Consider, for example, the waltzes in *The Merry Widow*.)

Adelaide, the feisty runaway wife, performs a character-defining number in each act: "Jim" in act 1, "I'm Through with Roaming Romeos" in act 2, and "The Dixiana Rise" in act 3.[12] Replete with dotted rhythms and syncopations, these moderate-tempo numbers are as much dances as they are songs. The lyrics for "Jim" imply a torch song, for Adelaide bemoans not seeing her husband for twenty-three years, even though it was she who left him. While it anticipates *Show Boat*'s "Bill" in sentiment, it definitely foreshadows the music of Broadway's most famous Adelaide, the *Guys and Dolls* heroine whose fourteen-year engagement has given her a permanent cold. Like her *Guys and Dolls* counterpart who sings "Adelaide's Lament," this Adelaide wishes that her marital situation would change—she would like to be with her husband again. She affirms this in "I'm Through with Roaming Romeos," a song in which she expresses her desire to stop leading a flirtatious lifestyle and settle down with one man. Through these two songs, the audience learns of Adelaide's change of heart over the past twenty-three years—the songs amplify the plot and provide further insight into Adelaide's psyche. This close union of song and plot was unusual in a musical comedy of the time. Adelaide also knows about current social dance, as she demonstrates in "The Dixiana Rise," where she tells of a new step of the same name, and refers to many other dances in the course of the number, including the one-step, turkey trot, Highland fling, tango, and buck-and-wing. Adelaide is no shrinking violet and experiences life to the fullest. Elizabeth Murray, who created the role, garnered tremendous praise for her extraordinary performance.[13]

Chi-Chi is featured in two engaging numbers, "Chi-Chi" and "The Bubble." "Chi-Chi," marked "quasi Schottische," is an energetic and playful duet for Chi-Chi and Dick that captures the effervescent spirit of the entire show; "The Bubble" is an expansive lyrical number sung as Chi-Chi is trying to reunite Dick and Sylvia. Even though she is a minor character, Chi-Chi sings two of the score's highlights.

Whereas *High Jinks* includes French and American characters and is set in France, *Katinka* has a cast of Russians, Americans, and Turks and takes place in three different cities: Yalta, Old Stamboul, and Vienna.[14] The show, set just before World War I (which was taking place in Europe when the show opened), begins with the wedding of Katinka and Boris Strogoff, the Russian ambassador to Austria. Katinka, whose name means "pure," is marrying Boris out of duty to her mother, for she really loves Ivan Dimitri, Boris's attaché. Thaddeus Hopper, an American friend of Ivan's, helps Katinka escape to Turkey, where act 2 takes place "on a street in Old Stamboul," to quote the playbill. Ivan and Boris's servant Petrov have gone there looking for Olga, the ambassador's first wife, who chose to live as a slave in a harem rather than remain with her husband. If Olga is alive, Boris's marriage to Katinka would have to be annulled on grounds of bigamy. Hopper and Katinka arrive, as does Mrs. Helen Hopper, who is missing her husband, especially since it is their wedding anniversary. Glad to see her husband, she is confused about Katinka's presence. Thaddeus, meanwhile, has arranged for Arif Bey to come to his rooms, take Katinka, and hide her in Izzet Pasha's harem until the marriage crisis is resolved. Of course Bey mistakenly kidnaps Mrs. Hopper and takes *her* to the harem. Herr Knopf, who is opening a Turkish café in Vienna, comes to the harem looking for girls to employ at his establishment and leaves with Helen. The third act takes place at Knopf's Turkoise-in-Vienna café. All the principals are gathered when Olga appears and reveals her identity. The romantic entanglements quickly unravel as Katinka and Ivan reunite and the Hoppers reconcile.

In *Katinka*, characters are defined through their music even more than they are in *High Jinks*. The principal lovers, Katinka and Ivan, sing lush, nearly operatic music, evident in their soaring and emotive waltz duet "'Tis the End," which appears near the end of act 1. Ivan displays his lyrical singing in "Katinka," a ballad in which he extols the merits of the title character, and the romantically evocative "My Paradise." Katinka's waltzes, "One Who Will Understand" and "I Want All the World to Know," with their high, sustained notes, are conceived for a classically trained soprano. But Katinka must also be able to sing in a lighter style for "Rackety-Coo," a love song about pigeons during which a flock of birds was released onto the stage. The song recalls "Willow, Tit-Willow" from Sir W. S. Gilbert and Sir Arthur Sullivan's *The Mikado* (1885) in both musical style and avian theme, though this one ends happily.

By contrast, Mrs. Hopper's music is in the style of American musical comedy, befitting the fact that she is American. "I Want to Marry a Male Quartet" is replete with dance-inspired syncopations and dotted rhythms. As implied in the title, a male quartet accompanies Mrs. Hopper in the comic song. In "Your Photo," Mrs. Hopper implores her husband to hurry home, not because she misses him but because the picture she has of him is nasty and chilly against her bosom. The ragtime-derived musical style of both songs distinguishes her from Katinka, whose music consists largely of European-style waltzes. Even "Rackety-Coo," Katinka's lighter song, does not follow the syncopated style of Mrs. Hopper's music.

Olga, Boris's wife, whose existence allows Ivan and Katinka to be together, sings what became one of the show's most famous songs, "Allah's Holiday." The number, meant to establish the Turkish setting of act 2, begins with a verse whose minor mode, thin texture, and extremely languid melody differentiate it from the other music in the score. The major-mode refrain, marked "Andantino," continues this wistful atmosphere through a gently rising motif that begins most phrases. Harbach's lyrics for the opening of the refrain, "Sounds of silver cymbal, tambourine and timbal," further amplify the song's implicit exoticism.

High Jinks and *Katinka* both transferred to London. *High Jinks* opened at the Adelphi Theatre on August 24, 1916, where it ran for 383 performances, longer than it played in New York. Because the show appeared in London during wartime, producer Alfred Butt was concerned about the Germanic-sounding names of its creators and so changed them to Roderick Freeman (for Friml) and Ogden Hartley (for Harbach).[15] Eventually, Butt removed even these pseudonyms from the playbill because of his intense fear that any Germanic overtones would damage the show's revenues and success. *Katinka* opened at the Shaftesbury Theatre on August 30, 1923, long after it had closed on Broadway, and played for 108 performances.

To speak in broad terms, *High Jinks* followed precepts of musical comedy and *Katinka* followed operetta principles, but neither was a pure example of one approach or the other. *High Jinks*'s French setting, as opposed to an American one, placed it closer to operetta, while the time period of both works—the near present—was characteristic of musical comedy. No actual time frame is given for *High Jinks*, but it is implied that the story takes place shortly before the outbreak of war in Europe in 1914, and *Katinka* is set, according to the authors, just before the war. Mention of the actual war had to be avoided in the librettos, since these shows were escapist entertainments. Furthermore, their European settings had to be portrayed as safe places for Americans to travel.

Americans appear as foreigners in both shows. Adelaide in *High Jinks* and Mrs. Hopper in *Katinka* perform similar musical comedy–style numbers that distinguish them from their European counterparts. Likewise, Americans instigate the principal action of both plots: Dick brings a perfume to Thorne in *High Jinks*, and Thaddeus Hopper arranges Katinka's escape from Boris in *Katinka*. Americans were of course central to musical comedy but were more often seen at home than abroad.

Oriental exoticism and the lure of Asia as an enticing region of mystery also feature prominently in both shows. The High Jinks inhalant originates in Tibet, act 2 of *Katinka* takes place in Old Stamboul, and "Allah's Holiday" became one of *Katinka*'s hits because of its exotic flavor. Westerners exert "control" over aspects of the Orient in both cases—an American captures the perfume and brings it to France in *High Jinks*; Herr Knopf establishes his own Turkish café in Vienna. This idea of Western authority over the Orient, presented here in microcosms, follows the basic tenets of Orientalism as a Western imperialist discourse, an idea formulated by Edward W. Said in his seminal work on the topic.[16] Orientalism was a recognizable theme in American popular musical culture at the time; it appeared in such Tin Pan Alley songs as Irving Berlin's "In My Harem" (1913) as well as in revue numbers, including Sigmund Romberg's "Ragtime Arabian Nights" from *The Passing Show of 1914*. Friml and Harbach, therefore, by including Orientalist features in these works, were part of a wider cultural discourse on the topic.

Madcap Comedies

Between *Katinka* and *Rose Marie*, Friml's focus was on musical comedy. Stories were set in the present day, though not always in New York City, and often involved either some sort of mistaken identity (sometimes self-perpetuated) or meddling friends and family members. Two Friml shows appeared in 1917: *You're in Love* (February 6, 1917, Casino Theatre, book and lyrics by Otto Hauerbach and Edward Clark), a shipboard comedy in which sleepwalking heroine Georgianna's thrice-married aunt tries to thwart her niece's marriage plans, and *Kitty Darlin'* (November 7, 1917, Casino Theatre, book and lyrics by Otto Hauerbach and P. G. Wodehouse), a bedroom farce that was a vehicle for Alice Nielsen, the operetta star-turned-operatic soprano for whom Victor Herbert wrote *The Fortune Teller* (1898). Future Broadway legend, lyricist, and librettist Oscar Hammerstein 2nd garnered his first Broadway credit in *You're in Love* as assistant stage manager. Produced by Arthur Hammerstein, Friml's show provided the younger Hammerstein's entrée into the world of musical theater on Broadway.

The next season's *Sometime* (October 14, 1918, Shubert Theatre, book and lyrics by Rida Johnson Young) was, on the surface, about a woman who tells the story of her love life in flashback. The show's biggest appeal, though, were the performances of stage luminaries Mae West and Ed Wynn. *Glorianna* (October 28, 1918, Liberty Theatre, book and lyrics by Catherine Chisholm Cushing) is the tale of a young woman who poses as a widow in order to help a friend, whose husband has gone missing and is supposedly dead, gain access to his fortune. Complications ensue when the husband shows up alive and well. *Tumble In* (March 24, 1919, Selwyn Theatre, book and lyrics by Otto Harbach), described on the playbill as "A Comic Rhapsody in Two Raps and Four Taps (Musical Comedy in Two Acts, Four Scenes)," is a fast-paced farce set in a fashionable home during a burglary. The unfortunate intruder must remain hidden and witness the various plot antics, including an imposter bride and the arrival of the "real" wife, a psychic who thinks the burglar is a spirit, the visit of a meddlesome alcoholic aunt, and a proactive quarantine, just in case the butler has smallpox.

Notions of social class unify the final set of pre–*Rose Marie* shows. *The Little Whopper* (October 13, 1919, Casino Theatre, book by Otto Harbach, lyrics by Bide Didley and Harbach) and *June Love* (April 25, 1921, Knickerbocker Theatre, book by Otto Harbach and William H. Post, lyrics by Brian Hooker) both feature female leads whose lies about who they really are and their social standings get them into trouble. *The Blue Kitten* (January 13, 1922, Selwyn Theatre, book and lyrics by Otto Harbach and William Carey Duncan) concerns a French waiter who, ashamed of his real job, poses as a successful newspaper editor to his immediate family. Matters go awry when his daughter falls in love with one of the restaurant's wealthy patrons. Finally, *Cinders* (April 3, 1923, Dresden Theatre, book and lyrics by Edward Clark) is a modern retelling of the Cinderella story. These latter two rags-to-riches tales would have had special resonance for Friml, for they were his story: growing up the son of a poor baker in Prague, he was now in the early 1920s a successful—and relatively wealthy—Broadway composer.

Throughout this series of nine shows, Friml employed various musical styles to amplify different dimensions of love. In *You're in Love*, for example, Auntie Payton elaborates her distrust of the male gender in the juicily titled "Keep Off the Grass," and Georgianna and her fiancé, Hobby, bemoan Auntie's stipulation that she will not allow their marriage to take place unless they promise to avoid physical contact for one year in the semi-comic "A Year Is a Long, Long Time." These songs are both in typical musical comedy style and are filled with syncopations and dotted rhythms. However, not every song about love has negative connotations; two extol the joys and merits of love: the waltz "Love Land" and the gentle ballad "You're in Love." Friml emphasizes dotted rhythms and syncopations in songs that accentuate the uncertainties of love while diminishing, though not completely eliminating, them in numbers that reflect its surety.

In *Sometime*, whose story shifts between the present and the past, the title song, a waltz, links the two temporalities. In the previous year's *Maytime*, with music by Sigmund Romberg and book and lyrics by Rida Johnson Young, the waltz "Will You Remember" appears in each act to unify the multigenerational storyline. Young brought her knowledge of the effectiveness of this technique to "Sometime," a song that serves the same basic function. A sequence of wistful sixteenth-note anacruses provides an immediate dreamlike evocation in the opening of the refrain on the words "Somewhere, somehow, sometime, someday," creating a fine musical-textual effect.

Enid, the storyteller of *Sometime*, is supposed to marry Henry Vaughan, but the voluptuous Mayme (played by Mae West) has other ideas. Mayme puts innocent Henry into an embarrassing situation that causes Enid to postpone the wedding until her fiancé completes a five-year "good behavior bond." In the end, Enid and Henry marry, and Mayme is left to her own vices. Enid and Mayme are radically different women, and Friml used music to accentuate this dichotomy. Whereas Enid sings the waltz "Sometime" as her principal number, Mayme dazzles the audience with the sexually suggestive "Any Kind of Man." It was in this song that Mae West introduced the shimmy to Broadway. The dance, which involved a horizontal shaking of the upper body, especially the shoulders, became immensely popular and was quickly associated with female sexual seductiveness.[17]

Friml said he was reluctant to write for Mae West because of her sultry walk, which he called "something between a strut and a shimmy." He even told Arthur Hammerstein that he "didn't write that kind of music," referring to the style associated with striptease. But after meeting West, Friml decided that she was a real lady and gloated over the fact that she stopped the show every night with his music.[18]

Tumble In presents two different views of marriage, one positive and one negative. In act 1, Dallas Brown, eager to marry Anne Wilson, sings the duple-meter ballad "You'll Do It All Over Again." The song is notably void of dotted rhythms and syncopations and is a metrically (and tonally) solid account of how even though marriage may be difficult, it becomes obvious, as time passes, that it would be worth it to "do it all over again." The opposite view appears in "The Wedding Blues." Here, Jim, Anne's overweight brother who must be married if he is to keep his generous allowance from his soon-to-arrive aunt, needs his friend Kitty McNair to impersonate his wife, Bella, who left him because he was too fat. Dal resolves that Kitty and Jim need a small ceremony to commence the charade, and the faux couple express their aversion to marriage in "The Wedding Blues." Here, dotted rhythms and syncopations pervade the refrain. As he had done in *You're in Love*, Friml used syncopation or the lack thereof to distinguish between contrasting impressions of marriage.

This treatment continues in *The Little Whopper*. In Harbach's book for the show, Kitty Wentworth, a pupil at the privileged Arlington Academy, is engaged to George Emmett and secretly plans to elope with him before he leaves on a U.S. diplomatic mission to Brazil. She involves herself, her friend Janet MacGregor, and Jack Harding, one of George's friends, in her scheme, a plan that becomes increasingly complex due to her telling all sorts of lies, or whoppers. Kitty fabricates a story about needing to visit the Adamses, imaginary family friends who are visiting from Boston, so that she can meet up with George. She ends up having to play Mrs. Adams while Jack becomes Mr. Adams. While the fictional Adamses are spending the weekend with Janet MacGregor and her parents, George arrives at the house for business with Janet's father, only to discover his fiancée "married" to someone else.

In "It's Great to Be Married," Jack and Kitty, posing as the fictitious Adamses, sing about married life. Dotted rhythms and syncopations characterize the musical style and accentuate a nonromantic, utilitarian view of marriage. According to the lyrics, once you're married, romance fades. This is not a lyric to be set to a romantic waltz, and its somewhat disheartening message matches Friml's jagged melody. Of course, the characters who sing it are not in love, so lush, romantic music would not be appropriate to the storytelling.

Kitty then sings "Bye Bye My Hubby" to Jack. Sung to an imposter husband, the lyrics give an off-putting view of marriage, for Kitty tells Jack that she needs to leave him in order to elope with the man she loves, George. Its marking of "allegro scherzando" and plethora of dotted rhythms accentuate Kitty's comic-driven anxiety to escape her lie-induced situation and marry her fiancé. By contrast, her song "If You Go I'll Die" is a heartfelt plea to George. In this impassioned waltz, chromatic appoggiaturas and passing tones emphasize her genuine anguish over the possibility that her fiancé will leave her since he thinks she is already either Mrs. Adams or Mrs. Harding. The absence of syncopated features in this song, which are characteristic of Kitty's music when she is lying, is an aural indicator that she is now, for once, telling the truth.

June Love is the tale of June Love, an attractive, young Long Island widow who wants to marry Jack Garrison. He thinks she is married, but once he learns she is not, he proposes to her. The show includes several romantic waltzes, including June's "Dear Love, My Love." By contrast, the vampish Belle Bolton of Broadway, a theatrical descendent of *Sometime*'s Mayme, sings the enticing "The Flapper and the Vamp" accompanied by "the boys." This song's emphasis on dotted rhythms indicates a character very different from June, specifically a sexually predatory woman, a vamp. In the song, Belle, thanks to lyricist Brian Hooker's clever use of rhyme, defines a flapper in somewhat ironic terms, calling her a vamp who is "emotional and sexual and highly intellectual."

In these shows, Friml establishes a trope for musically depicting love. True love is expressed through waltzes, finely crafted melodies that often are reprised later in the show. Foils to true love likewise appear in musical comedy–style numbers. By either following or avoiding these tropes, which audiences would have recognized, Friml realized that he could manipulate and to some extent control a show's musical-dramatic effect through musical style.

Certainly not everything in these shows revolved around depictions of love: single songs, stars, and subject matter also were distinguishing elements. *You're in Love* included an impressive sleepwalking song for Georgianna in act 2, "I'm Only Dreaming." Marked "quasi gavotte," showers of falling arpeggios accompany the languid melody, and obbligato parts for solo flute and violin are added in the final refrain, creating a chamber-like intimacy. The song follows in the tradition of Vincenzo Bellini's opera *La Sonnambula* (The Sleepwalker, 1831) and prefigures famous Broadway dream sequences such as those in Kurt Weill's *Lady in the Dark* (1941) and Rodgers and Hammerstein's *Oklahoma!* (1943).

Ed Wynn, a veteran of vaudeville and Ziegfeld's *Follies* (and who played jovial Uncle Albert in the 1964 film musical *Mary Poppins*), joined the cast of *Sometime* to provide comedic star power. He rewrote parts of the libretto, supplying some lyrics for himself to sing, and, more important, brought his stage persona to the fore under the guises of various secondary characters.[19] His presence in the show, along with that of Mae West, made *Sometime* among the longest-running productions of the 1918–19 theatrical season.

Body image is a central theme to *Tumble In*. Jim Wilson, the male protagonist, is obese, and his excessive weight is the reason his wife left him. Friml had previously addressed obesity through another Jim, Jim Jeffreys, the overweight American who goes to Dr. Thorne for weight-loss treatment in *High Jinks*. When these shows opened in the second decade of the twentieth century, idealizing the human body was a significant dimension within American popular culture. This was the time of Eugen Sandow, the "father of modern body building" who was promoted by Florenz Ziegfeld, and of magician and escape artist Harry Houdini. Edgar Rice Burroughs's *Tarzan*, with its depiction of a lean, muscular male physique, first appeared in 1912 and was followed by a series of popular sequels. This was also an era when eugenics (selective breeding) appeared in the news. Regarding the female body, beach bathing beauty contests were on the rise, leading to the famous beauty pageants of the 1920s.[20] These views of the body are evident in *High Jinks* and even more in *Tumble In* through their negative portrayals of certain body types. It was also a period of new and fashionable diets and weight-loss regimens. Jim Jeffreys was fulfilling the desires of many Americans at the time by seeking medical treatment for being overweight.

Curiously, another musical about obesity, *The Melting of Molly*, opened on December 30, 1918, almost three months earlier than *Tumble In* and in the same theatrical season. Sigmund Romberg wrote the score to the musical comedy in which a woman gains weight while her fiancé is away and goes to a weight-loss specialist when she learns he is returning. In the end, she sheds her unwanted pounds and, when her fiancé arrives, rejects him because he has gained weight!

Tumble In had further significance for its librettist and lyricist, for this was the last time that Otto Hauerbach used his given name professionally. As a direct result of anti-Teutonic feelings at the time, Otto Hauerbach, with his Germanic surname that had already been disguised as "Hartley" for the London production of *High Jinks*, formally changed his stage name to Otto Harbach. It was this name that he used for the remainder of his career.

From 1912 through 1923, Friml amassed significant critical acclaim. He received strong praise for his inaugural effort, *The Firefly*, and the accolades kept arriving. Although an unnamed *New York Times* critic was not impressed with the book for *Kitty Darlin'*, he cited Friml's music as doing "valiant service in sustaining the performance. It is varied and melodious—worthy of much better things."[21] For *Cinders*, the *Times* critic wrote, "Mr. Friml has never written more tuneful music. None of his tunes is cheap—and the air of distinction throughout is happily unmarred by a striving for the pseudo-operatic."[22] Friml was emerging as a significant Broadway composer, one who created his best music for classically trained singers but who was likewise able to write effective musical comedy numbers. His exceptional talent was in making the two styles complement each other in the same work.

Other Theatrical Projects

During the second and third decades of the twentieth century, Friml's music also appeared in productions alongside that of other composers. While his work on these shows did not necessarily garner him the fame and publicity of his complete scores, they nonetheless are important in his creative legacy, for they provided him with the opportunities to write for specific performers and to work with the legendary Florenz Ziegfeld.

Friml wrote four songs for *The Peasant Girl* (March 2, 1915, 44th Street Theatre), an adaptation of Oskar Nedbal's Viennese operetta *Polenblut* (Polish Blood) that starred Emma Trentini. *The Peasant Girl* not only had the same star as *The Firefly* but also the same basic plot, a rags-to-riches tale of an aspiring opera singer. Many Central European operettas were adapted for American audiences during the first quarter of the twentieth century, and *Polenblut* was part of this theatrical market. Especially during and immediately after World War I, Central European works held great nostalgic power, for they depicted a prewar world, a settled, picturesque Europe that was now part of the illusory world of the imagination. Many of the overt Viennese and Germanic plot references were excised since the United States was fighting Germany and Austria, and music was similarly altered or replaced to reflect American popular music styles as opposed to those of traditional Central European operetta.

The Peasant Girl included a great deal of Nedbal's original music. Common practice involved mixing old and new music in adaptations, and this is what happened in this show. Friml created two solo numbers for Trentini, "The Heart of the Rose" and "After the Rain—Sunshine," and the duet "The Flame of Love" for Trentini and her operatic costar, John Charles Thomas. Especially noteworthy is "The Heart of the Rose" with its splendid waltz refrain in which the singer must negotiate a vocal range of more than two octaves and sustain a high tessitura. Friml's other contribution to the score was the gavotte "Love Is Like a Butterfly," a number for the secondary leads.

Two editions of the *Ziegfeld Follies*, those of 1921 (June 21, 1921, Globe Theatre)—the one that was hailed as "the best of them all"[23]—and 1923 (October 20, 1923, New Amsterdam Theatre), featured Friml's music. As was typical practice, many composers contributed music to the revues. In 1921, the legendary Fanny Brice introduced "Second Hand Rose" (by Grant Clarke and James Hanley) and W. C. Fields inaugurated his recurring character of "The Professor." One of Friml's contributions to the score was "Bring Back My Blushing Rose," with lyrics by Brian Hooker, with whom Friml later wrote *The Vagabond King*. The song included solo parts for various roses: one white, one yellow, one pink, one red, and a rosebud, its theme thus anticipating "Only a Rose," the principal love duet from *The Vagabond King*.

Friml contributed two songs to the musical comedy *Dew Drop Inn* (May 17, 1923, Astor Theatre): "We Two" and "Goodbye Forever," the second co-written with Alfred Goodman, the show's principal composer. Robert Halliday, who became one of the decade's leading operetta stars with his stunning performances in Romberg's *The Desert Song* (1926) and *The New Moon* (1928), sang both songs with his costar Mabel Withee. Romberg wrote the ensemble music for *Dew Drop Inn* and would have heard Halliday's renditions of Friml's songs; perhaps they even inspired his writing for the Broadway baritone later in the decade.

Friml's Operetta Contemporaries

Friml was one of three great luminaries in the operetta genre, the other two being Victor Herbert and Sigmund Romberg (1887–1951). Herbert, the Irish-born and German-trained senior statesman of American operetta when Friml came on the scene, was known for his dazzling virtuosic scores, such as *Naughty Marietta*. Friml's scores have the same sort of demanding vocal parts for their principals but demonstrate a much wider array of additional styles. Friml's experience writing solo piano pieces of assorted types proved extremely valuable when he began writing for Broadway.

Romberg, like Friml, was a European immigrant. Born in Hungary to an upper-middle-class Jewish family, Romberg did not have Friml's formal conservatory training. After attending a music gymnasium in Osijek (today in eastern Croatia near the Hungarian border), Romberg went to Vienna and worked in the theater as a coach-accompanist, where he received tremendous practical experience regarding how musical theater operated. Romberg arrived in the United States in 1909, but it was not until 1914, two years after Friml made his Broadway debut with *The Firefly*, that Romberg began working on Broadway, first as a staff composer for the Shuberts, for whom he wrote music for revues (most notably their *Passing Show* series), musical comedies, and operetta adaptations. His first complete original operetta was the highly successful *Maytime* (1917), with words by Rida Johnson Young. Because of World War I, all references to the original German work, Walter Kollo's *Wie einst im Mai* (As Once in May), and its original music were excised, giving Romberg the opportunity to create an entirely new score.

Romberg and Friml each had their strengths. Romberg excelled at Viennese waltzes, a style near and dear to his heart because of the years he had spent in Vienna. Friml, growing up in Prague, would not have been as enamored with Viennese idioms as Romberg. Friml's conservatory training, experience with solo piano miniatures, and extraordinary improvisational skills gave him a surer compositional technique than that of Romberg, whose practical education in the workings of the theater and exposure to Viennese operetta gave him the advantage over Friml when it came to transforming Continental operetta into a distinctly American genre. For both composers, the early decades of the twentieth century led to the pivotal year of 1924, when each created an operetta that forever changed the musical theater: Friml's *Rose Marie* (September 2, 1924, Imperial Theatre, 557 performances) and Romberg's *The Student Prince* (December 2, 1924, Jolson's Theatre, 604 performances), the two longest-running Broadway musicals of the decade.

Coda: *An Experiment in Modern Music*

In the same year that these two landmark operettas opened, one of the most famous concerts of the twentieth century took place. On February 12, 1924, at Aeolian Hall, Paul Whiteman's *An Experiment in Modern Music* featured the world premiere of George Gershwin's *Rhapsody in Blue*. Whiteman organized the concert to prove that jazz-inspired music had come of age. Immediately before *Rhapsody in Blue* was a segment titled "Adaptation of Standard Selections to Dance Rhythms." Friml's "Chansonette" concluded this section, which also included a version of Edward MacDowell's "To a Wild Rose" (1896).

"Chansonette" was an arrangement of "Chanson," a solo piano piece from 1920. Conceived in D-flat, the work was published in both its original key as well as a transposed version in C. Besides the technical differences of requiring the pianist to play mostly on either black keys (D-flat version) or on white keys (C version), the timbre differs between the versions: the black keys offer a subtler effect; the white keys, a bolder one.

Ferde Grofé, who orchestrated *Rhapsody in Blue* (and who was also a fine composer in his own right; his *Grand Canyon Suite* (1929–31) was extremely popular in the third quarter of the twentieth century), arranged the number in 1922, calling it "Chansonette" and publishing it in *Schirmer's Library of Classics*. The arrangement was extremely popular with restaurant and hotel orchestras and was featured on Whiteman's concert as an example of successfully adding "dance rhythms" to works that did not originally have them. Grofé's orchestration includes a solo heckelphone (a bass oboe) that features prominently at the beginning of the arrangement. Ross Gorman, a member of Whiteman's orchestra, played heckelphone (along with saxophone, clarinet, and other reed instruments), hence Grofé's reasoning for including the unusual instrument in his arrangement.

"Chansonette" appeared in MGM's film of Noel Coward's *Private Lives* (1930), which starred Norma Shearer and Robert Montgomery. Near the end of the balcony scene (act 1 in the stage play), the orchestra plays the tune from below as Amanda (Shearer) and Elyot (Montgomery) discuss travel and confess to each other that they are still in love and want to be together. Earlier in the film, they remark that the orchestra has a small repertory, referring to a waltz. "Chansonette" also fits into this modest choice of music, a direct reference to its popularity. In 1923, another version of "Chansonette" appeared, this time a song published by Harms. Dailey Paskman, Sigmund Spaeth, and Irving Caeser added romantic lyrics to Friml's haunting melody.

"Chansonette" remained popular in its various guises, but in 1937, it was catapulted to unprecedented fame in the MGM film *The Firefly*. MGM's music director, Herbert Stothart, created a new accompaniment and transformed the gentle miniature into a lively foxtrot while Chet Forrest and Bob Wright added new lyrics of a quasi-Spanish flavor. Thus, "The Donkey Serenade" was born. (See chapter 6 for more on *The Firefly* film and "The Donkey Serenade.")

According to Friml himself, he came up with the melody for "Chanson" while indulging in one of his favorite pastimes, sleeping in a movie theater.[24] The tune that came to him in a dream ended up being one of his most memorable creations. It is fitting that the tune achieved perhaps its greatest success as the basis for "The Donkey Serenade," introduced in a cinema with darkened lights, the very type of venue in which Friml conceived it.

3 | Envisioning the West:
Rose Marie

IMAGES OF THE West and its indigenous peoples are among the most recognizable American icons. In the twentieth century, many novels, poems, plays, films, television shows, and even theme-driven tourist sites promoted, and to varying degrees invented, the geographical domain. Earlier writers also embraced the virtually unknown region, fabricating it when actual knowledge was not available (and sometimes even when it was) and choosing it as the setting for some of their most significant works.

Among the most prolific of these authors was the German novelist Karl May, who wrote around thirty western fantasies, even though he never traveled to the places he so vividly described. His books sold more than 100 million copies in German, and translations appeared in many other languages, including Czech and English. His heroes included a German-born adventurer named Old Shatterhand and the Apache chief Winnetou. Winnetou epitomized the "noble savage" and for Europeans embodied the American West. According to Libor Sikl, owner of Sikluv Mlyn, a Wild West theme park in the Czech Republic, "Every Czech knows Winnetou. He is the most famous character there is."[1] In American literature, Owen Wister's novel *The Virginian: A Horseman of the Plains* (1902), with its cowboy hero, also enjoyed tremendous popularity. And "Buffalo Bill's

Wild West" shows, which ran from 1883 to 1916, were enormously influential in promoting the West and its peoples.

During the 1920s, movies became another means through which the American West was depicted. It was in this decade that films became cultural institutions and hence emerged as central forces for image making and the creation of public perceptions about a myriad of topics.[2] In many Hollywood films, white interpretations were imposed on indigenous peoples; in *Nanook of the North* (1922), for example, Inuits are falsely depicted as living within a grand illusion of innocence, completely unaware of the world outside their own.[3] Another important film was the 1926 epic *The Vanishing American*, which concerned the Navajo during World War I.[4] Among the issues raised in this film were progress, imperialism, industrialization, race relations, Euro-American political and military supremacy, and Manifest Destiny (westward expansion and the promotion of American-style democracy).[5] Through the medium of film, Hollywood creators endorsed a wider phenomenon whereby native cultures were treated as museum pieces, monuments from a disappearing past.[6]

On June 2, 1924, exactly three months before the premiere of *Rose Marie*, Native Americans who were born within the geographic boundaries of the United States were granted American citizenship. Literature, film, and real life thus collectively contributed to a strong presence of Native Americans in the American psyche during the 1920s.

Into this cultural framework came *Rose Marie*, with its Canadian Rockies setting and assorted white and indigenous characters.[7] Like *Nanook of the North* and *The Vanishing American*, *Rose Marie* depicts native peoples from a white perspective. As with the characters in *Nanook of the North*, some of them are innocents, unaffected by the trappings of Western industrialization. And like those who would appear in *The Vanishing American*, the First Americans in *Rose Marie* are subjugated to ideas of Euro-American supremacy, racism, and imperialist attitudes.

An important stage precedent for *Rose Marie* was *Tiger Rose* (October 3, 1917, Lyceum Theatre), billed as "a melodrama of the great Northwest." Written by Willard Mack and produced by David Belasco, the story concerned flirtatious Rose Bocion, a French-Canadian "hellcat" or "tiger," hence the play's title. Rose safeguards her lover, Bruce Norton, who committed murder and is being pursued by Constable Devlin, a Canadian Mountie. The same storyline is at the heart of both *Tiger Rose* and *Rose Marie:* a leading lady named Rose is in love with a man wanted by the Mounties (but in *Rose Marie*, the accused murderer is in fact innocent).

Belasco's involvement with *Tiger Rose* infused the production with a strong sense of dramatic realism, including an onstage thunderstorm that was one of the play's most memorable moments. Belasco, one of the most important Broadway personalities in the early twentieth century, was active as an actor, writer, director, and producer. He was dubbed "the Bishop of Broadway" not only because of his trademark ecclesiastical-like attire but also because of his extremely powerful position in the theatrical world. Stage realism was of paramount importance to the legendary impresario. Belasco insisted on "natural" lighting effects, historically accurate costumes, lifelike sets, and an unaffected and spontaneous acting style.[8] His approach to the theater in general and the Pacific Northwest in particular, as seen in *Tiger Rose*, strongly influenced *Rose Marie* and its underlying sense of dramatic realism.

The original idea for *Rose Marie* had nothing to do with the depiction of indigenous cultures. Producer Arthur Hammerstein heard about a weeklong event in Quebec whose visual focal piece was an ice palace atop a hill overlooking the city. At the end of the festivities, revelers supposedly climbed the hill wearing snowshoes and carrying torches. When they reached the summit, they melted the palace. Arthur sent his nephew Oscar and Otto Harbach to Montreal to research the matter, only to find that the destruction ceremony that would have constituted the new show's climax did not exist.[9] This discovery kept the producer from pursuing the idea of an ice palace show. The trip was not in vain, however, for Harbach and Hammerstein saw numerous First Nations people in Canada, experienced French Canadian culture firsthand, and decided that these had the makings of an operetta.

When Friml heard that Arthur Hammerstein was planning a new musical on an Indian theme, he contacted the producer about providing the music; after all, Friml had enjoyed a critically and commercially successful collaborative relationship with Hammerstein and Harbach during the previous decade. Friml, Dvořák's student in Prague, knew of his teacher's exhortation to his American students to look to their own indigenous musics for inspiration. And having enjoyed success with his "Indian Song" in Prague, he was ready to embark on a full-scale musical that included Native American elements.

But when Hammerstein told Friml that in order to work on the new project he would have to write the score with Herbert Stothart (1885–1949), since the veteran musical comedy composer had already been signed to create the show's music, Friml's enthusiasm wavered. Friml and Stothart did not get along, and Friml had refused to work with Stothart on *Cinders* the previous year. However, Friml overcame his misgivings, even though he found it difficult to collaborate with Stothart.

According to Friml, when he joined the creative team, Arthur Hammerstein wanted the show to feature Metropolitan Opera star Mary Ellis (1897–2003) in the title role and had already contracted Stothart to write the score. When Ellis saw the music Stothart wrote for her, she refused to sing it because she did not think it was good enough. Even though Stothart's name appears throughout the vocal score as either composer or co-composer for many numbers, including the famous "Totem Tom-Tom," Friml, in his unpublished memoirs, strongly asserts that Stothart had nothing to do with the final version of *Rose Marie*. He also relates how Stothart's name remained on the published score, even though the earlier composer's songs were omitted: "Herbert Stoddard [*sic*], who wrote the music to two comedy songs for 'Rose Marie'—and they were not very significant numbers—went to Schirmer Publishers and had his name put on each of my compositions from 'Rose Marie' when he did not lift a pen to write a note of my music. He also collects royalties on the sheet music even though he wrote nothing except the two comedy songs which I eventually threw out of the show because they were inconsistent with the theme and high tenor of the show. They distracted from the high level of the music."[10]

Friml also claimed that Harbach had already completed the book and lyrics for *Rose Marie* when the producer signed his nephew Oscar to work on the show. (Young Oscar, however, had traveled with Harbach to Quebec and helped formulate the show's content.) Friml avowed that Hammerstein did not write any lyrics for *Rose Marie*, though the budding lyricist-librettist did ask a lot of questions of Harbach about how to create a show. He could thus be considered an apprentice to the experienced Harbach and received valuable practical training from a noted wordsmith. Although the playbill and published materials for *Rose Marie* suggest that Friml, Harbach, Stothart, and Hammerstein co-wrote the score, they belie the truth, at least according to Friml, who stated, "in simple words—Otto Harbach and Rudolf Friml wrote the show which is named 'Rose Marie.'"[11]

Rose Marie opened at the Imperial Theatre in New York on September 2, 1924, where it played an impressive 557 performances. In the 1920s, only Sigmund Romberg's *The Student Prince* (book and lyrics by Dorothy Donnelly), with 604 performances, ran longer. Mary Ellis and Dennis King (1897–1971), an English dramatic actor, starred as the romantic leads.

Ellis, an experienced opera singer who created Suor Genovieffa in the world premiere of Puccini's *Suor Angelica* (1918), triumphed in *Rose Marie*. She went to Hollywood in the 1930s, where she made three films for Paramount Studios before moving permanently to London. There, she became a West End favorite and starred in Jerome Kern's *Music in the Air* (1933) and Ivor Novello's *Glamorous Night* (1935) and *The Dancing Years* (1939). Although she retired from the stage in 1970, she continued to appear on television as late as 1994, when, at the age of ninety-seven, she played opposite Jeremy Brett in *The Memoirs of Sherlock Holmes*.[12]

Critics adored Ellis in *Rose Marie*. Deems Taylor wrote, "She is, in fact, utterly charming. She has vivid beauty and vitality that combine to make her always interesting to watch, and her voice is even better than it was in her Metropolitan days. Its upper register is clear, without a suspicion of shrillness, its lower notes are warm and expressive, and she uses it well."[13] Heywood Brown wrote that Ellis had "the precise sort of voice for which musical comedy has been yearning," and Alan Dale stated, "She sings deliciously, and is not too grand opera. The poor gell has of course an operatic education to battle with, but she will successfully overcome it."[14]

Ellis's costar, Dennis King, starred in productions of Shakespeare and Anton Chekhov plays before venturing into the realm of musical theater. *Rose Marie*, his first musical, changed the course of his career. King became Friml's most successful leading man, for he also created the lead male roles in *The Vagabond King* and *The Three Musketeers* and starred in the 1930 film version of *The Vagabond King* opposite Jeanette MacDonald (1903–65). King also played Gaylord Ravenal in

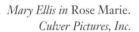

Mary Ellis in Rose Marie.
Culver Pictures, Inc.

the 1932 revival of *Show Boat* and created the role of Count Palaffi in Rodgers and Hart's *I Married an Angel* (1938), where he introduced the show's title song. Decades later, he appeared as Emperor Chang in Cole Porter's television musical *Aladdin* (1958). King was known for his operatic voice, good looks, and strong stage presence, the requisite traits for a successful operetta leading man.

Rose Marie opens in Lady Jane's Hotel in Saskatchewan, where Rose Marie LaFlamme works as a chanteuse in the saloon. Two men enter looking for Rose Marie: Hawley, one of her suitors, and Émile, her brother. The proprietress informs them that she is probably with the miner Jim Kenyon, a response that does not please either of them. Native American Blackeagle is drinking in the saloon when his wife, Wanda, arrives and begins flirting with Hawley. Herman, Lady Jane's fiancé, introduces himself with a comic character–defining number ("Hard-Boiled Herman"), at the end of which Jim, the romantic lead, enters. Jim, whose nickname is "Wild Jim" because of his zest for drink, women, and song, tells Sergeant Malone of the Canadian Mounties that he has changed his lifestyle since having fallen in love with Rose Marie and begins literally to sing her praises ("Rose Marie"). The Mounties make their way to the saloon and enter singing a march ("The Mounties"). Rose Marie times her entrance to join them in their final refrain.

Rose Marie tells Émile that she has been on a sleigh ride with Jim and confesses her love for him ("Lak Jeem"). Malone responds to this news by telling Rose Marie how much he loves her, usurping Jim's song ("Rose Marie") and using it as an expression of his affection. Wanda, jealous of all the interest bestowed on Rose Marie, wants men to pay attention to her and invites Hawley to her home, suggestively telling him that Blackeagle is drunk and won't return for several days.

Jim and Rose Marie, left alone, confess their love in the famous "Indian Love Call." Rose Marie tells Jim the story of the song—an Indian boy called to his Indian girl from the top of a hill, and if she responded, it meant that she would be his wife. She teaches him the song, which he of course learns quickly.

The scene shifts to Wanda and Blackeagle's cabin, where Hawley arrives, finding Wanda alone, as she had promised. Jim, who has been settling a land claim with Blackeagle, innocently arrives at the cabin to deliver a map when he discovers Wanda and Hawley in a compromising situation. He quickly departs, but just then, Wanda and Hawley notice Blackeagle watching them through the window. Blackeagle confronts Wanda, she kills him, and Hawley and Wanda, trying to figure out what to do and both wanting to destroy Rose Marie and Jim's relationship, decide to frame Jim for the murder.

At the Totem Pole Lodge, Émile tries to convince Rose Marie that she should marry Hawley and forget about Jim, since Hawley could buy her lots of things and Jim could not. Rose Marie and the girls contemplate this idea ("Pretty Things") when Wanda and Hawley enter, telling everyone that Jim has killed Blackeagle. Jane and Herman, though already engaged, finally admit their mutual love ("Why Shouldn't We?"). Rose Marie decides to go to Quebec and marry Hawley (after all, she does not want to marry a murderer), and Wanda begins the operetta's lavish production number, "Totem Tom-Tom."

Jim, not knowing that he is wanted for murder, comes to tell Rose Marie that he has received an offer to work in a Brazilian mine and invites her to come with him. He tells her that he is going to "their" cabin, and if she does not want to join him in Brazil, she should sing "Indian Love Call" and he will go on his own. Rose Marie, realizing that Jim must be innocent, decides to travel with him and tells Hawley and Émile that she will not be going to Quebec. At that moment, Malone arrives and arrests Jim for Blackeagle's murder. Hawley, knowing the truth, offers Rose Marie a deal: if she will marry him in Quebec, he will tell Malone to stop tracking her lover and allow him to cross the U.S. border to freedom. Rose Marie realizes that the only way she can save Jim is to accept Hawley's offer as she reluctantly sings "Indian Love Call."

The dramatic context of the song at this point in the show is reversed from Rose Marie's explanation of its origin. According to Rose Marie, singing "Indian Love Call" signifies that the lovers will be together, while in the act 1 finale, its function is exactly the opposite. The reason for this anomaly stems from the creators' desire to include a reprise of "Indian Love Call" while also forcing the lovers to separate. Dramatic continuity suffered in order to have Rose Marie sing "Indian Love Call" and also to ensure that the lovers were not together at the end of the act.

Act 2 takes place one year later. Lady Jane has moved to Quebec, married Herman, and opened a fancy-goods shop ("Only a Kiss"). Rose Marie is about to marry Hawley, who, being a Francophile, wants the bridesmaids all to wear Breton folk costumes. During the wedding festivities ("The Minuet of the Minute," "Door of My Dreams"), Jim storms in, furiously towing Wanda, to prove his innocence. Rose Marie will have nothing to do with him, thinking he deserted her (even though by singing "Indian Love Call," she communicated with him that she was not going with him to Brazil). Disconsolate and wishing he could forget Rose Marie (scene 2 finaletto), Jim departs. Wanda, ever the opportunist, then tries to blackmail Hawley but ultimately is forced to tell the truth about Blackeagle's murder, her tryst with Hawley, and Jim's innocence. Rose Marie, with a reawakened love for Jim, sings "Indian Love Call" and leaves in search of her true love. Jim, sitting alone outside "their" cabin, bemoans Rose Marie's marriage to Hawley and sings "Indian Love Call" as he recalls his past happiness. When he hears Rose Marie respond from the distance, his mood brightens, and the operetta ends with the reunited lovers still singing "Indian Love Call," this time to each other.

The Music of *Rose Marie*

Rose Marie is not pure musical comedy, quintessential operetta, or full-blown opera. It defies such easy categorization. Musical comedy is apparent in the secondary pair of lovers, Herman and Lady Jane. Their mannerisms, lyrics, and music provide counterpoint to the high-intensity saga of Jim and Rose Marie. Operetta is present in the generally lush musical treatment, especially evident in the waltzes and marches. Classical opera makes its appearance through technically complex writing in numbers such as the act 2 finaletto. The overall serious nature of the show also points toward opera, especially the verismo style associated with Puccini, Ruggiero Leoncavallo, and Pietro Mascagni. Passions are heightened, and an onstage murder is central to the plot. Add depictions of Native Americans to this already eclectic mix, and the result is something extraordinarily innovative, especially since the divergent elements work together to tell the story and accentuate many of its subtleties.

Just as defining characteristics of musical comedy, operetta, and opera appear in *Rose Marie*, so do elements foreign to each genre. Murder and revenge are not common in either musical comedy or operetta, nor are such extreme emotion and intense musical drama. Syncopated "popular" numbers likewise are rarities in serious opera.

The show's creators viewed the work as a unified musical-dramatic entity, even putting the famous statement into the printed program that "the musical numbers in this play are such an integral part of the action that we do not think we should list them as separate episodes. The songs which stand out, independent of their dramatic associations[,] are 'Rose-Marie,' 'Indian Love Call,' 'Totem Tom-Tom,' and 'Why Shouldn't We?' in the first act and 'The Door of My Dreams' in the second act."[15] Such a statement is not unique to *Rose Marie*, for similar ones also appear in other shows from the decade, including Rodgers and Hart's *Chee-Chee* (1928).

What did the creators mean by placing this declaration in the playbill? Should it be taken literally, especially when titles for individual musical numbers appear in the vocal score? Friml and Harbach were certainly striving for musical-dramatic unity. This was a show in which every song would relate to the plot. Even the big production number, "Totem Tom-Tom," is couched within the fundamental narrative. *Rose Marie* is not a series of complex musical-dramatic scenes, as the statement implies, but rather is constructed largely of distinct musical numbers separated by spoken dialogue. Perhaps Friml, Harbach, and Hammerstein were distinguishing this show from revues, and to a lesser degree from musical comedies, where songs and story were not so intrinsically linked.

Rose Marie's operatic influence is most apparent in the act 2 finaletto, a musical highpoint scored for Rose Marie, Jim, Hawley, Émile, Ethel (a friend of Hawley's), and Wanda. Although called a sextet, since it features six singers, it is in musical reality only a quintet, for Ethel and Wanda sing the same line. (Neither Ethel nor Wanda needed to be cast with strong singers.) This number, which incorporates spoken dialogue, recitative, and arioso (a style between recitative and flowing melody) before the climactic contrapuntal ensemble, occurs at a dramatic highpoint in the plot: Rose Marie feigns an open declaration of her love for Hawley, forcing Jim to leave. The onstage principals join him in expressing his regret as he leads them in singing "All I ask is that I may forget you." Friml ably demonstrates his solid knowledge of polyphonic vocal writing in the passage, recalling, albeit in an abridged manner, great operatic ensembles such as the act 2 finale of Mozart's *The Marriage of Figaro* (1786) and the sextet from Gaetano Donizetti's *Lucia di Lammermoor* (1835).

Rose Marie and Jim, as the romantic leads, sing vaulting, lyrical, and technically challenging music and are the characters whose vocal styles, more than any other, make this work an operetta. Rose Marie's music includes two luscious waltzes, act 1's "Lak Jeem," her introductory solo number, and act 2's expansive "The Door of My Dreams," which includes the chorus. She also leads the chorus in act 1's "Pretty Things," a wistful song about how a man can win a woman's heart by giving her "pretty things."

Jim's most important solo is "Rose Marie," a duple-meter ballad in which he extols the merits of the title character. Friml's "hook" in the refrain is the short-long rhythmic motif introduced at the end of the first phrase: "Oh, Rose **Ma**-rie, **I love** you" (short notes are in bold). Later in the act, in "Pretty Things," Rose Marie sings the same distinctive figure several times. She has thus entered his musical—and psychological—world, knowing subconsciously that while he may not give her expensive objects, he will give her something more valuable: love.

In contrast to the music of Rose Marie and Jim, that of Lady Jane and Herman follows musical comedy conventions. Their songs can be almost speech-sung; in fact, Friml occasionally demands this performance style by not indicating pitches, only rhythmic values, as in the refrain of Herman's "Hard-Boiled Herman." It is not until the female chorus repeats the passage that the actual melody is heard. Ragtime-derived syncopations, metric anticipations (accented syllables occurring before a strong beat), and dotted rhythms, devices that Friml successfully employed in his musical comedies from the previous decade, fill Herman and Jane's music. This is especially evident in their duet "Why Shouldn't We?," during which they express the joys of being in love. Harbach's textual references to animals being in love—"Even the pollywogs down in the crick / Birds in the forest and fish in the sea"—anticipate those of Cole Porter's well-known "Let's Do It, Let's Fall in Love" (1928): "Birds do it, bees do it, even educated fleas do it."

Musical comedy also appears in the act 2 trio for Herman, Jane, and Malone, "Only a Kiss," a lighthearted number about various types of kisses. Beginning with a waltz section marked "Con massimo sentimento (*mock ballad*)" and paro-dying the notion of waltzes being love songs (which is exactly what Rose Marie's waltzes are), the trio also includes a foxtrot and later a tango. Harbach's lyric even mentions Rudolph Valentino, the Argentine film star who popularized the tango and its sexual associations (and who was acquainted with Friml). The Valentino reference rooted the plot in the 1920s and certainly would have resonated with audiences.

These two fundamental approaches, operetta and musical comedy, meld in the anagrammatically titled "The Minuet of the Minute," the duple-meter bal-lad for Rose Marie, Herman, and chorus that begins the wedding sequence. Rose Marie sings in a lyrical style, befitting operetta, while Herman's music is replete with dotted rhythms and rests, evoking musical comedy. Rose Marie and Herman each present their own melody individually in their own refrains (the orchestra plays Rose Marie's melody underneath Herman's) before they join together for the third refrain, each singing their own line.

"The Minuet of the Minute" can be read as a testimony about the state of operetta in 1924: Friml and Harbach show an almost prophetic self-awareness about the new directions this particular show would forge. Rose Marie calls the minuet "quaint" and "old-fashioned," adoring these qualities of tradition. She represents European-derived operetta. Herman responds by telling her how "we sway in dances of today" to music with an exaggerated ragtime influence, show-ing the power of American syncopated styles. By having Rose Marie and Herman sing their contrasting lyrics and music at the same time, the show's creators dem-onstrate that the two approaches can work together to fine dramatic and musical effect. Although an actual wedding does not occur within the plot of *Rose Marie*, this number is truly a marriage number, for it celebrates the union of operetta and musical comedy, a courtship Friml, Harbach, and Arthur Hammerstein had begun a dozen years earlier with *The Firefly*.

The fourth musical style in the score, the Indianist one, is the one for which *Rose Marie* is best known. Musical images of Native Americans have existed since the sixteenth century, and among those that Friml would have surely known were his teacher Dvořák's Symphony no. 9, "From the New World" (1893), and Victor Herbert's opera *Natoma* (1911).[16] Friml was well aware of the basic musical taxonomy for sounding "Indian," an aural palette that included chromatic melodies, drone fifths repeated to sound like drum beats, long-short-short rhythmic motifs, and harmonic stasis.[17] Friml did not do anything especially innovative in creating an Indian sound world in *Rose Marie* but rather assimilated and capitalized upon known and perhaps even somewhat clichéd musical devices.

"Indian Love Call" is undoubtedly the most recognizable song from *Rose Marie*. The famous "calling" motif, with its ornamented descending figure and chromatic passing tones, appears at the onset. Intoned on the neutral syllable "ooh," the "call" itself establishes an immediate sense of timelessness and mystery. This sense of removal from the present continues in Rose Marie's verse (beginning "When the lone lagoon"), which opens with a so-called gypsy or Hungarian scale (C-D-flat-F-E-C) and whose first cadence lands on an augmented triad. These unusual tonal features evoke a sense of the Other, which in this case, because of the lyrics, is applied to Native Americans. The melodic doublings at a third below in the opening line of the refrain ("When I'm calling you") further establish the song's exotic languidness. Later, trademark repeated fifths in the bass appear on the final words of the phrases "That means I offer my love to **you**" and "If you refuse me, I will be **blue**" (words in bold are those under which the fifths are sounded). In "Indian Love Call," Friml creates a general flavor of the musical Other, for the only prominent specifically Indianist features are the repeated drone fifths. Take away these fifths, along with the song's lyrics, title, and dramatic context, and the music that remains could be extremely effective and evocative in a variety of situations where musical difference is the goal.

This is not the case with "Totem Tom-Tom," where Indianist features permeate the music. The lavish showpiece is a diegetic number in the operetta, that is, one that is a performance within the performance, for it is set as an entertainment outside the Totem Pole Lodge. Repeated drone fifths, strongly articulated repeated notes within pentatonic melodies, and a slitheringly chromatic countermelody provide the aural backdrop for the choreographic spectacle. The chorus, dressed as totem poles, dance and hop around the stage, led by the murderess

"Totem Tom-Tom" from Rose Marie. *Culver Pictures, Inc.*

Wanda. They tell of an ancient ritual that has fallen into legend and memory, endorsing the idea that creators of the 1920s were relegating Indians to the past. The lyrics insult and demean Native Americans, collectively portraying them as lazy drunkards, and thereby pose challenges when reviving the show.

Wanda, the seductress, has her own theme, called "Wanda's Theme" in the score, that distinguishes her from the remainder of the cast. Since Wanda's only prominent vocal solo in *Rose Marie* is in "Totem Tom-Tom," this instrumental moniker identifies her the rest of the time. Marked "Lento e molto misterioso," the theme consists of a three-note melody stated initially in parallel minor chords over repeated throbbings in the bass meant to evoke the sound of the tom-tom. The motif features prominently in the underscoring for the cabin scene in act 1, the melodrama (spoken dialogue over music) that culminates in Wanda's murder of Blackeagle.

Before leaving the music of *Rose Marie*, mention must be made of its stunning male chorus. The male chorus became a standard feature in American operetta of the 1920s through its appearance in both *Rose Marie* and Romberg's *The Student Prince*. Male choruses became associated with themes of community in operetta, and more often than not, they sang marches about fighting for justice and overcoming tyranny and oppression. This is precisely the treatment the chorus receives in *Rose Marie*, for they are the Mounties, the noble Canadian law enforcers. Their recurring song, "The Mounties," is a stirring march with a lyric about capturing wrongdoers. In its first appearance, Sergeant Malone, the leader, is onstage, while the chorus begins offstage. The men sing from a distance, causing the audience to experience them first as disembodied voices whose initial impression is made aurally rather than visually. Malone sings the central part of the ABA form march as a solo, then the chorus enters, joining with Malone for the reprise of the opening material. (In the final statement of the refrain, Rose Marie joins the men, prefiguring Kathie's songs with the male chorus in *The Student Prince*.)

Dramaturgical Issues

Rose Marie is a fundamentally serious musical with comic interludes. Three sobering themes pervade its dramatic fabric, all of which reflect social attitudes of the mid-1920s: interracial romance, portrayals of Indians, and views of women and sexuality.

Interracial romance is cleverly and conveniently averted in *Rose Marie*, although it is suggested. Rose Marie's exact racial background is ambiguous in the libretto, complicating the notion of whether or not she and Jim are an interracial couple. Some writers argue that Rose Marie has mixed Indian-white ancestry and spent her childhood in Canada before going to France to live with her grandmother.[18] Considering that *Rose Marie* appeared before *Show Boat* and its poignant miscegenation scene and well before *South Pacific* (1949) with its diatribe on racism ("You've Got to Be Carefully Taught"), the insinuation of an interracial romance in *Rose Marie* is certainly noteworthy.

Closer examination, however, belies this notion, for Rose Marie is almost certainly French Canadian. Just before the act 2, scene 1 finale, Rose Marie explodes at Jim for what she perceives is his treatment of her, alluding to her self-inferiority regarding her ethnicity: "You think you make fool of little Canadian girl. . . . It is little Canadian girl who laugh at you." (Harbach wrote Rose Marie's part with a phonetic French accent.) Earlier, when she tells Jim the legend that forms the basis of "Indian Love Call," she says, "De Indians teach dat call to me when I am a little girl" (act 1, scene 2). Since she refers to Indians in the third person, she does not appear to include herself among them.

French connections are evident not only in her name but also in her brother, Émile, who reminds her in the opening scene, "A long tam ago when come to France to bring you to Canada—what you promise Grandmamma Forchette?" Later, she tells Hawley that her grandmother is in Bretagne (act 1, scene 5). So, making the heroine French shrewdly averts an interracial romance, although she has adopted many of the ways of Native Americans. Rose Marie "went native," so to speak.

The sexual relationship between Wanda and Hawley articulates the opposite side of the coin. Theirs was a carnal, even animalistic desire. This was undoubtedly an interracial liaison, and, as portrayed in the musical, could not and did not have any true love behind it. It resulted in the murder of Blackeagle and an unfounded murder charge for Jim. According to the message in *Rose Marie*, this is what happens when there is an interracial romance—ruin and devastation.

First Nations peoples in *Rose Marie* are treated as either gallant primitives or sexual villains. This follows their polarized Hollywood portrayal in *The Vanishing American*, where they were either "noble children of nature" or "vicious savages."[19] Neither view is accurate or complimentary. Colonialist discourse and ideas of white self-superiority, the "white man's burden," are clearly evident. Michael J. Riley, in discussing the 1925 silent epic *The Vanishing American*, asserts: "[I]ndigenous peoples are embodiments of antiquated lifeways and, hence, are rendered as emblematic of the past, rather than as viable participants in the world of the present."[20] The same could be said for *Rose Marie*. Native Americans were part of the romanticized past, the realm of operetta. They cohabited nicely with the people of Ruritania, the quintessential operetta domain, in the vivid world of the imagination.

The good-bad view of Native Americans is readily apparent in the portrayals of Rose Marie and Wanda: Rose Marie (whose ethnicity is unclear but certainly possesses Native American traits) is the "noble child of nature" who loves the outdoors and its allure, while Wanda is the "vicious savage" who commits murder. This dichotomy also reflects the various depictions of women and sexuality in the show.

Malone describes Rose Marie as being "tame as a sparrow" when compared to other women Jim Kenyon has known. She is also the romantic, telling Jim the tale of two Indian lovers that results in "Indian Love Call." Furthermore, she is resolutely monogamous, as she asserts in her song "Lak Jeem." Just before the ensemble version of "Indian Love Call" (act 1, scene 5), Rose Marie reminds Émile that when she was a little girl, she promised to sing the song only to the man she would marry. She remains true to her word.

Wanda is the antithesis of the title character. Whereas Rose Marie is virtuous, Wanda is the sexually provocative "primitive" who murders her husband. She is portrayed as morally depraved because of her promiscuity. Her character has roots in the title character of Georges Bizet's *Carmen* (1875): both women have different moral attitudes from the mainstream European ones, and both use physical gesture, including dance, as a means to display their sensuality.

A third female, Lady Jane, offers yet another view of femininity and sexuality. In act 1, she runs a brothel. Her antics as a madam are given a comic spin, providing a foil to Wanda and her sexual exploits. Because Jane is white, her activities are condoned, but when Wanda engages in identical behavior, she is considered amoral. The differing dramatic interpretation of the same act practiced by two distinct women is racially determined. Lady Jane, being white, is allowed to express her sexuality, but Wanda, being non-white, is not. This racial profiling is especially curious in that it is the opposite of what one would expect in the 1920s, when a white woman's overt sexuality onstage was *not* condoned, whereas it would be a character-defining trait of an exotic female. Friml and Harbach thus were challenging established societal norms of sexual behavior in *Rose Marie*.

Performance Legacy

The popularity of *Rose Marie* extended well beyond North American shores. On January 25, 1925, Hammerstein and his wife, Myra, and children, Billy and Alice, sailed for London, where they remained for three months while he supervised the show's London production.[21] The musical ran for two years at the Theatre Royal, Drury Lane, opening there on March 20, 1925, and playing for a magnificent 851 performances. The production starred Edith Day, a leading British actress of the time, at Hammerstein's suggestion.[22]

The famous incident of the sweet English soprano auditioning for Day's understudy has become musical theater lore. She read the first line of the refrain of "Indian Love Call"—"When I'm calling you—oo-oo—oo-oo-oo"—and innocently intoned, "When I'm calling you, double *o*, double *o*."[23] Although she did not get the part, she immortalized the line.

After London, Myra and the children returned to the United States while Oscar went to Paris, where he spent six weeks working on the show's French production.[24] This proved to be time well spent, for the Paris production turned out to have the operetta's longest run at 1,250 consecutive performances. The production, which opened at the Théâtre Mogador on April 9, 1927, was lavish in every respect and boasted multiple mountain scenes, an exotic Totem Pole Hotel, a "maison de couture" with its own mannequin parade, and a sumptuous Quebec ballroom.[25] It set new standards for opulence in French musical theater, and, due to numerous revivals, the show remains a staple of musical repertory in

France. The work's title was slightly altered as well for Paris: a hyphen was added, making it *Rose-Marie.*

The operetta continued to play elsewhere in Europe. The Paris production (in French) transferred to Germany (March 30, 1928, ad Rideaumus, Admiralspalast) and Hungary (March 31, 1928, Budapest, Király Színház), where it opened on successive evenings. The first German-language production appeared at the Brussels Stadttheater on January 28, 1933.[26]

Rose Marie has been revived many times in many places and remains one of Friml's most popular works. The composer even wrote three new songs for the revival mounted by the Los Angeles and San Francisco civic opera associations in 1950: "Whenever Night Falls" (lyrics by Otto Harbach), "The Waltz-Song" (also known as "I'm in Love with a New World," lyrics by Forman Brown), and "Mam'selle" (lyrics by Forman Brown).

Film Versions

With its amazing stage success, it is no surprise that *Rose Marie* was transferred to the silver screen. Three film adaptations of the operetta exist, all from MGM: a 1928 silent version starring Joan Crawford; a 1936 black-and-white version featuring Jeanette MacDonald and Nelson Eddy; and a 1954 color version with Ann Blyth, Howard Keel, and Fernando Lamas. Each film incorporates various aspects of the stage original but manipulates them to the particular needs of the individual films and their overall aesthetics.

In the 1928 revised version, whose title includes a hyphen, Rose-Marie (Crawford) is a free-spirited young woman who captures the hearts of all the men in a mountain trading post. She falls in love with the mysterious Jim Kenyon (James Murray), who arrives at the post and soon is accused of murdering a trooper. In order to save Jim, Rose-Marie agrees to marry Etienne Doray (Creighton Hale), the effeminate son of the post's most prominent citizen. Sergeant Malone of the Mounties, meanwhile, goes in pursuit of the real murderer, Black Bastien (Gibson Gowland). Jim is exonerated of the murder charges, Rose-Marie breaks off her engagement to Etienne, and the couple is free to plan their future together.[27]

In 1936, audiences were treated to a sound version of *Rose Marie,* the plot of which was again substantially altered, this time to be a vehicle for "America's Singing Sweethearts," Jeanette MacDonald and Nelson Eddy. The duo achieved tremendous fame in the previous year's *Naughty Marietta,* and *Rose-Marie* (again with a hyphen in the title) was the second of the eight film collaborations of "The Beauty and the Baritone."[28]

The film was especially important for Nelson Eddy, for it was in *Rose-Marie* that his iconic image as a man in uniform, a Mountie in this case, was established. He donned various military uniforms in his later films, including *Girl of the Golden West* (1938), *Balalaika* (1939), *New Moon* (1940), and *Northwest Outpost* (1947), the last with a score by Friml. No matter what Eddy did after *Rose-Marie*, he was always the stoic Mountie for whom duty, honesty, and honor were paramount. Although his acting was somewhat stilted, his singing elicited cheers and squeals.[29]

Film adaptations of Broadway musicals during the 1930s frequently had a substantially altered plot (when compared with the original), and the music was often radically changed. What worked well onstage did not always transfer successfully to the screen due to the differences between live theater and the film medium. Changes also needed to be made in order to trim a three-hour live production into a film of roughly half the length and also to showcase studio stars.

Rose-Marie followed these maxims. In the screenplay by Frances Goodrich, Albert Hackett, and Alice Duer Miller, Montreal opera star Marie de Flor (Mac-Donald), who drops her first name "Rose" in her stage name, goes in search of

Jeanette MacDonald and Nelson Eddy in the 1936 film Rose-Marie. *Copyright John Springer Collection / Corbis.*

her brother, John Flower (James Stewart), who has escaped prison and murdered a Mountie. Also pursuing Flower is Sergeant Bruce (Eddy) of the Mounties. (Bruce's surname is the same as that of Rose's murderous lover's first name in the play *Tiger Rose*. Also following the lead of *Tiger Rose*, Rose Marie loves a murderer—here it is her brother rather than her lover.) The diva and the Mountie fall in love and sing "Indian Love Call." Bruce's duty wins out over his passion, however, and he leaves Marie in order to arrest her brother. Marie, meanwhile, returns to Montreal and resumes her opera career. While singing the title role in *Tosca*, she suffers a nervous breakdown and loses all will to recover until Bruce arrives, singing the "Indian Love Call" and taking her in his arms.

Only four songs from the original stage play made it into the film: "The Mounties," "Rose Marie," "Totem Tom-Tom," and "Indian Love Call." Friml, with lyricist Gus Kahn, wrote a new ballad, "Only for You," for Eddy, while Herbert Stothart, the film's musical director, and Kahn created the lighthearted "Pardon Me, Madame" for MacDonald.

Other new music for MacDonald included opera arias and popular songs, befitting her character in the film. In the opening sequence, when Marie is onstage at the Royal Theatre in Montreal, MacDonald sings "Juliette's Waltz" and the death scene from Charles-François Gounod's *Romeo and Juliet*, with Allan Jones as Romeo. MacDonald had strong aspirations to be an opera singer, something she realized largely by interpolating opera arias into many of her operetta films.

In the middle part of the film, Marie, while looking for her brother, sings in a dance hall. Her music in this sequence includes the interpolated "Dinah" (by Harry Akst, Sam Lewis, and Joe Young) and "Some of these Days" (by Shelton Brooks). She obviously could not sing opera arias in a dance hall but sings her popular songs in an operatically trained way. The dance hall audience loses interest in Marie's rendition of "Some of these Days," so the proprietor has Belle (Gilda Gray) take over in a belt style. Throughout the film, Marie is a practitioner of "high culture." Here, this role is emphasized by contrasting her vocal style with that of Belle's.

Toward the end of the film, MacDonald and Jones sing excerpts from act 3 of Puccini's *Tosca*. After Cavaradossi (Jones) is shot and Tosca (MacDonald) realizes that he was hit with real bullets and not blanks, as she assumed, Marie hears a non-synchronized "Indian Love Call" in her mind's ear. Of course the voice that sings it belongs to Sergeant Bruce. Both Tosca and Marie experience mental anguish that is depicted through music: Tosca's by Puccini and Marie's by Friml. It is one of those wonderful instances where two levels of storytelling (the opera and the film) intertwine and dramatic realities blur.

Eddy saw Jones as a threat to his role as the male singing star of *Rose-Marie*. In the final opera sequence, Jones originally sang "E lucevan le stele," an impressive tenor aria from *Tosca*. After Eddy saw the film in previews and realized that Jones was singing the last big solo number, he threatened to cause trouble if it was not cut. Eddy did not want Jones to be remembered as the last male singer heard in the film, and "E lucevan le stele" was excised from the final version.[30]

The 1954 version, which has an unhyphenated title, was the first musical to be filmed in color and CinemaScope, and producer-director Mervyn LeRoy took full advantage of the possibilities of the big screen. The Canadian Rockies locations are nothing short of breathtaking, and the physical geography is the film's greatest asset. The setting moved westward from its original Saskatchewan to Alberta and British Columbia.

With the setting, the story also changed. Now, Rose Marie Lemaitre (Ann Blyth) is a backwoods French Canadian trapper's daughter who loves James Severn Duval (Fernando Lamas), a mean-spirited trapper from the Yukon. Mountie Mike Malone (Howard Keel) searches for James on criminal charges, while the native girl Wanda (Joan Taylor) romantically pursues Malone.

The same four songs from the 1924 stage original that appeared in the 1936 film were kept in 1954. Busby Berkeley gave "Totem Tom-Tom" an unforgettable choreographic treatment with Taylor, as Wanda, leading a hundred braves in the foot-stomping dance. Friml, then in his seventies, teamed with lyricist Paul Francis Webster on three new romantic songs for the film: "I Have the Love," "The Right Place for a Girl," and "Free to Be Free." Combined with the one song Friml wrote for the 1936 film and the three for the 1950 stage revival, seven additional songs by the composer of the original stage version thus exist. Furthermore, the film's music director, George Stoll, and Herbert Baker created a humorous song for the comic character Barney McGorkle, played by Bert Lahr (the Cowardly Lion in 1939's *The Wizard of Oz*), "The Mountie Who Never Got His Man."

The Saga of "Indian Love Call"

As the most recognizable music from *Rose Marie*, "Indian Love Call" has a performance legacy of its own, independent of the show from which it came. The song often appears in unexpected and sometimes humorous places. "Über die Prärie" is a German-texted version of the song (published in 1953) that transfers its setting several thousand miles south. Arthur Rebner's lyric begins "Der Missouri rauscht / Ich halte Wacht" (The Missouri flows / I keep watch) and offers concrete geographic imagery that is closer to Karl May's Western novels than to Otto Harbach's evocative words. Mexican pop singer Jorge Negrete recorded the song in Spanish as "Amor Indio" in 1964, and the Mexican group Los Freddy's included it on their *30 Inolvidables* album in 2003.[31]

Among the most famous versions are those by Artie Shaw and Slim Whitman. Shaw's 1938 swing interpretation propelled the song to fame among jazz musicians and fans in the years immediately before World War II. The romantic country singer and yodeler Slim Whitman garnered huge accolades for his rendition of the song; "Indian Love Call" was the number one country song in 1952, indicating its popularity in yet another musical style.[32]

Whitman's version appeared in the Tim Burton film *Mars Attacks!* (1996) to great comic effect. In a parody of both alien invasion movies and films that include a cavalcade of big name stars, Slim Whitman's "Indian Love Call" saves the Earth. The Martians' heads explode (literally) when they hear the rendition, and the grandmother offers the pithy statement as to the cause of the aliens' distress: "I think it must be my music."

The song receives a passing mention in the 2006 musical *Grey Gardens* (book by Doug Wright, music by Scott Frankel, lyrics by Michael Korie) in the number "The Five-Fifteen."[33] In this scene, set in 1941, Edith Bouvier Beale is rehearsing for a recital that she plans to give as part of a reception to honor her daughter Edie's engagement to Joseph Patrick Kennedy Jr. She asks her pianist, "What's next on the bill, 'Indian Love Call'?," indicating that she was intending to perform Friml's song on her attention-grabbing concert. (She does not sing "Indian Love Call" in the musical but rather the newly composed "The Mysterious Orient," a song, like "Indian Love Call," tinged with exoticism.)

"Indian Love Call" also found its way onto formal concert programs. Considering Friml's background as a classical pianist, this full-circle treatment is completely warranted, especially considering the popularity of Indianist-inspired works on concert stages. Maurice C. Whitney prepared a concert paraphrase for piano solo in 1948 that is still played today. Opera singers were also drawn to the work's inherently engaging qualities. Dame Joan Sutherland recorded it in 1966 with Richard Bonynge and the New Philharmonic Orchestra in an arrangement by Douglas Gamley.

The song's Canadian associations made it the perfect choice for a love song in the 1999 *Dudley Do-Right*, a parody of the animated television character.[34] In the film, the narrator refers to "Indian Love Call" as "that famous old Mountie movie song." Its first appearance is when Nell (Sarah Jessica Parker) sings it to Dudley (Brendan Fraser) to prove she is who she claims to be. He responds to her invocation, establishing the song's role in the film as a symbol of their enduring love. This is similar to the song's function in the stage play. "Indian Love Call" appears several times in the course of *Dudley Do-Right*, including one particularly comic episode after the title character gets hit on the head. In every instance, it is intentionally sung poorly—the film is a zany comedy, after all, not an operetta.

In addition to the specific uses of "Indian Love Call" mentioned above, *Rose Marie*, with its exotic imagery, overly zealous Canadian Mounties, and ardent love songs, is filled with prime material for parody. Rick Besoyan's *Little Mary Sunshine* (November 18, 1959, Orpheum Theatre) was a full-scale takeoff on the classic operetta.[35] Set in the Colorado Rockies, Mary Potts, who runs the Colorado Inn, is saved from the treacherous Yellow Feather by her hero, Captain "Big Jim" Warrington of the Forest Rangers. The show's big love duet was the "Colorado Love Call," a direct play on Friml's "Indian Love Call." Its male choral march was "The Forest Rangers," a takeoff on "The Mounties."

Regarding the Mounties themselves and their overt masculinity, Monty Python's "Lumberjack Song" is the epitome of *Rose Marie* parody. The song first appeared on *Monty Python's Flying Circus* in 1969, when a distressed barber (Michael Palin) confesses his life dream: to be a lumberjack.[36] After Palin's initial lines, "I'm a lumberjack and I'm okay," the camera jumps to a chorus of Canadian Mounties who repeat the soloist's lines. The team maintains the marchlike quality and the alternation between soloist and chorus of the model, all while making fun of the song's noble lyrics. The chorus ultimately gives up on its hero, who soon sings of his desire to "wear women's clothing and hang around in bars" and ultimately to "be a girlie, just like my dear mama." This lampooning of not just "The Mounties" but of every overtly masculine operetta march is one of the classics of referential comedy.

4 | A Francophile Musical:

The Vagabond King

AMERICANS HAVE BEEN enamored with French culture since the eighteenth century. One of the highpoints of this love affair took place in the 1920s, when French literati were sought out as trendsetters and suppliers of conversation topics at high-class cocktail parties.[1] French cuisine, fashion, literature, art, and music were all at the forefront of American taste and sophistication during the decade.

In the years after the signing of the Treaty of Versailles, Paris was filled with expatriates, especially Americans. Americans went in droves to Paris, some to escape Prohibition and its stifling world, and others, who had served in Paris during World War I, to return for more of the city's delights.[2] As the title of a popular World War I song asks, "How ya gonna keep 'em down on the farm after they've seen Paree?"

In 1921, foreigners comprised 5.3 percent of the city's population, whereas in 1931, the figure had risen to 9.2 percent—nearly double what it had been a decade earlier.[3] In 1927, the American population in Paris numbered nearly forty thousand.[4] Why the influx? Paris played a major role in the American imagination of the 1920s. A "trip to Paris" was the dream of a lifetime. Henry James's assertion in the nineteenth century that France was "the foreign country *par excellence*" still rang true.[5] For Americans, the city was the mythological geographic embodiment of "public liberty, private liberty, high culture, and untrammeled sexuality."[6]

Artistic types congregated in Paris. Gertrude Stein was firmly established there, and among the other Americans who spent time in the "City of Lights" during the 1920s were writers e. e. cummings, F. Scott Fitzgerald, Ernest Hemingway, and George Orwell; painter Marsden Hartley; performer Josephine Baker; and composers George Gershwin, Cole Porter, Aaron Copland, and Virgil Thomson.

By this time, according to Patrice Higonnet in *Paris: Capital of the World*, the French capital had moved from myth to phantasmagoria. She distinguishes between the two and their approaches to the past and the present: "Myths are hard: phantasmagorias are soft. In myth, a presumed past is extended into a collective present which it simultaneously explains and complicates. In phantasmagoria, by contrast, an artificial present is excused by a distortion of current reality that is justified by simplification and embellishment of the past."[7] This "simplification and embellishment" is exactly what often takes place in the finest musical theater librettos, including that of *The Vagabond King*. Historical detail is simplified while interpersonal relationships are embellished.

The Vagabond King takes as its source material Justin Huntly McCarthy's play *If I Were King* (October 14, 1901, Garden Theatre), itself a tale appended to the real-life François Villon (1431–?), poet-hero of medieval France. The play was revived on Broadway several times before Friml's musical version debuted, including productions at the Lyric Theatre in 1908, Daly's Theatre in 1909, the Manhattan Opera House in 1913, and the Shubert Theatre in 1916. Furthermore, in 1920, Fox Film Corporation released a silent film adaptation starring William Farnum and Betty Ross Clarke. The numerous revivals and release of the film attest to the tale's sustained popularity in the early twentieth century.

Producer Russell Janney wanted to create an operetta based on *If I Were King*.[8] Janney and Friml had worked together on *June Love* in 1921, and the producer had tremendous respect for Friml's music. McCarthy, the play's author, agreed to the idea, although he thought Janney and Friml were foolish for attempting it. The playwright knew the challenges of creating a musical libretto, for he had co-written the book and lyrics (with David Stevens) for Victor Herbert's *The Madcap Duchess* in 1913.

Undaunted by McCarthy's advice, Janney called in another *June Love* collaborator, Brian Hooker (1880–1946), to help wordsmith W. H. Post with the libretto and lyrics. McCarthy's play lacked humor, and the creative team, knowing that this was an essential element of a Broadway musical, compensated by increasing the role of Tabarie and making Oliver, who had been an evildoer, a comic. Hooker, who taught English at Yale University and was known for his translation of Edmond Rostand's *Cyrano de Bergerac* and for adapting W. S. Gilbert's *Engaged* for the musical theater in 1925, increased the intellectual level of the show and ensured its historical authenticity.

Janney pushed Friml to write his best and would not settle for anything less. When Friml gave Janney a song that the producer thought could be better, he would quip, "I'll give this number to Ziegfeld—he won't know!" Janney's high standards paid off, for *The Vagabond King* was an unqualified success. The show opened on September 21, 1925, at the Casino Theatre, and played for 511 performances in its initial Broadway run.[9] Also successful in London, it opened at the Winter Garden Theatre on April 19, 1927, and played for 480 performances, followed by a tour and revivals in 1929, 1937, and 1943.[10]

Reviews were uniformly strong: critics and audiences alike adored the swash-buckling tale of heroism and chivalry. The *New York Herald-Tribune*'s critic wrote, "For playgoers who love tense drama and for playgoers who love operetta there is a deal of pleasure awaiting them at the Casino. . . . 'The Vagabond King' has about everything that an entertainment of this kind should have—a good story of romance and adventure, acted by actors who can act; a play draped in turn by the flaming dresses of the underworld and the gold and purple of royalty, and, through it all, an accompaniment of exquisite and gorgeous melody." Friml's music was also praised: "That Rudolf Friml found unusual inspiration for his music in the McCarthy drama we can well believe, because surely never before has his contribution to operetta risen to such lovely and such distinguished heights."[11]

The reviewer for the *New York Sun* noted the advances in dramatic realism that were affecting operetta and extolled the merits of the leading man, Dennis King, in this regard. "What a joy it is to find in operetta a leading man who can act! In these days of stage realism the singing voice is not enough. A manly presence is not enough. Acting is needed, and acting Mr. King supplied in full measure. . . . As the tavern bravo who worships a great lady and under her inspiration leads the people of Paris to victory against the Burgundians outside the walls of the city King caught something of the poetic flame of John Barrymore."[12] Friml agreed with this appraisal of King, stating that the actor "put the show over for me. There was nobody yet who could play or sing the part as well as Dennis King."[13]

If I Were King and its musical progeny, *The Vagabond King*, concerned the real-life French poet François Villon. Little is known of Villon's life, with the exception of his involvement with several criminal activities, among them a violent encounter with a priest, Philippe Sermoise (or Chermoye), that resulted in the latter's death and his participation in the theft of five hundred crowns from the College of Navarre treasury.[14] Villon was both a gutter poet, often writing on scatological themes, and an educated man, for he received his bachelor of arts from the Faculté des Arts at the University of Paris in 1449 and a master of arts in 1452.[15] He is best known for his *Testament*, a 2,023–verse masterpiece that provides astonishing insight into fifteenth-century Parisian life. Villon infuses his writing with remarkable vivacity, telling of taverns, drinking, and all manner of people in the French city.[16] As the noted Villon scholar David A. Fein asserts: "The great paradox of Villon's work . . . resides in the remarkable combination of universality and specificity that characterizes his poetry. On one hand, his work embraces certain fundamental aspects of the human condition—love and sexuality, suffering and violence, time and the aging process, mortality, and sin and redemption. . . . On the other hand . . . much of Villon's work remains firmly grounded in its historical context, tightly attached to specific sites, people, and events."[17]

Villon's life and work offered ideal source material for a musical theater work, for Villon is a hero who lives exuberantly and loves passionately. A story about Villon could include fervent love songs, heroic marches, large choral ensembles, and plenty of opportunities for musical characterization. Its fifteenth-century Parisian setting provided mouthwatering creative challenges for set and costume designers, and the resulting collective image of a phantasmagorical France captivated audiences.

The story opens in the Fir Cone Tavern, a venue filled with revelers, students, and prostitutes ("Life Is Like a Bubble in Our Glasses"). The inn is owned by Margot, a madam; one of the prostitutes in her employ, the rough and forthright Huguette, tells the tale of her profession ("Love for Sale") before confessing her passionate love for François Villon, "The Vagabond King."

A dramatic scene without music ensues as King Louis XI and his assistant Tristan enter incognito. They are looking for Villon in order to pacify the king, who is troubled by a dream he had. In the dream, Louis was a swine in the streets of Paris and found a "pearl of great price," which he put in his crown. The pearl shone all around, filling Paris with light just before a great star fell from heaven.

The quietly melancholic atmosphere is shattered as Villon enters to tremendous fanfare ("Song of the Vagabonds"). The title character affirms his loyalty to France and calls for the defeat of the enemy, Burgundy, before telling his audience about a noblewoman whom he saw praying and with whom he has fallen in love. As he tells the tavern's clientele about writing a poem for her, an image of Katherine De Vaucelles—the woman—appears upstage ("Some Day").

The mood shifts when Villon calls the king a nincompoop, after which Louis XI, still disguised, asks the "Vagabond King" if he could do a better job. Villon replies assuredly in the affirmative. Katherine arrives at the tavern, looking for her newfound poet to inform him that Thibaut d'Aussigny is preparing to betray France to Burgundy and to implore him to kill the traitor. She gives him a rose as a symbol of her love ("Only a Rose").

Thibaut enters the tavern, and Villon quickly defeats him in a swordfight. The king's Scotch Archers, however, hold Villon as Louis discloses himself and again asks the victorious swordsman if he really thinks he would make a better king than the reigning monarch. Villon replies by calling him "Louis Do-nothing, Louis Dare-nothing" and asserts that although he is a thief, he is a "king among thieves." Louis, angered by this response, orders that Villon be taken into custody. Katherine throws a rose to Villon, reminding him that she loves him.

Act 2 takes place in the king's garden. Louis is pondering Villon's line of poetry, "If Villon were the King of France," when Katherine and Lady Mary, her lady-in-waiting, enter. Villon arrives, bathed and clean-shaven, and the king introduces him as the Count of Montcorbier, the new grand marshall of France. Louis, jealous of the attention Katherine is showing toward Villon, gives him a choice: he can either be grand marshall and hold tremendous political power as "King for a Day," as long as he condemns himself to the gallows afterward, or

Duel between François Villon (Dennis King) and Thibaut d'Aussigny (Brian Lycan) from the original production of The Vagabond King. *Billy Rose Theatre Division, The New York Library for the Performing Arts, Astor, Lenox and Tilden Foundations.*

return to the streets. Villon chooses the former, and Louis, again thinking of Katherine, adds a provision: he can save himself if, within that single day, he can also gain Katherine's affections without revealing his true identity.

Prisoners from the Fir Cone Tavern come to be judged by the new grand marshall—only Tabarie recognizes him as Villon and is subsequently made Viscount de Tabarie, valet to the grand marshall. Huguette asks the grand marshall about Villon, confessing that she truly loves him. Montcorbier (Villon) orders the prisoners freed, and Katherine implores him to spare Villon's life, to which he replies that he has already done so, after which he asks her for the pleasure of her company ("Tomorrow").

The Herald of Burgundy arrives to wage war, and Villon, in his position of authority, tells him that a grand masquerade ball will take place that evening and they will be busy dancing and drinking. The witnesses to this event call him a fool, but Villon lets the decision rest. His undisclosed plan is to lure Burgundy to Paris and attack them at the city gates.

The masque opens act 3 ("Nocturne"). Oliver and Tabarie compete for Lady Mary's attention ("Serenade"), while Tristan expresses his outrage at the immense popularity of Villon's "Song of the Vagabonds." (This reference to the song informs the audience that it is a diegetic musical number and functions differently than most of the music in the score.) Noel, a member of the court, pursues Huguette, who refuses him ("Huguette's Waltz"). Katherine goes to the king's garden to meet Montcorbier, with whom she is falling in love, something she cannot explain since she still is devoted to Villon ("Love Me Tonight").

The king has hired a new astrologer to help interpret his disturbing dream, and Villon, wearing the king's robes, goes to meet the mystic, who is none other than the traitor Thibaut. The imposter astrologer tries to kill the person who he thinks is the king but who is really Villon in disguise. During the fight, Huguette lunges in front of Villon, taking a fatal wound and dying in her hero's arms ("Love for Sale" reprise). Villon confesses his true identity to Katherine as he leaves to defeat the arriving Burgundians.

Act 4 opens with a comic scene in which Oliver, Margot, and Tabarie prove that they are terribly inept at defending Paris, but the mood changes from humor to victory soon thereafter, for Villon enters, leading his band through the streets of Paris singing "Song of the Vagabonds." Amid the rejoicing, Villon passes the capital sentence upon himself, dampening the entire atmosphere. Louis declares that if any will take Villon's place on the gibbet, he will pardon the "King of the Vagabonds." Finally, Katherine arrives, carrying a rose, and says that she will marry Villon, thus making him her vassal and giving him life. Villon replies that a star has fallen to him from the heavens, and the king realizes that this was the meaning of his dream.

The Music of *The Vagabond King*

Producer Russell Janney, like his rivals Florenz Ziegfeld and J. J. Shubert, enjoyed seeing his name in lights. On opening night, Friml fully expected the electric sign on the Casino Theatre to read "Russell Janney's *The Vagabond King*" and was surprised and honored when it instead boasted "Rudolf Friml's *The Vagabond King*."[18] The producer knew that the operetta would be nothing without Friml's captivating score. *The Vagabond King* contains some of Friml's most famous songs, ranging from stirring marches ("Song of the Vagabonds"), ensemble numbers of various types (opening chorus, "Nocturne," "Scotch Archers' Song"), and character-defining songs ("Love for Sale," "Huguette's Waltz") to romantic ballads ("Some Day," "Only a Rose") and entrancing waltzes ("Love Me Tonight").

"Song of the Vagabonds" is one of the most memorable songs from any 1920s operetta. This march anthem is part of a long line of "songs of social injustice" in Broadway musicals, a tradition rooted in French protest songs of the late nineteenth century, the most famous of which is the "Internationale." One could almost call these numbers "songs that sound like the 'Internationale.'" "Song of the Vagabonds" followed on the heels of "The Mounties" in *Rose Marie* and predated similar dramatic numbers such as "Stouthearted Men" in Sigmund Romberg and Oscar Hammerstein's *The New Moon* and, later in the century, Claude-Michel Schönberg and Alain Boublil's "Do You Hear the People Sing?" from *Les Misérables* (1985).

The anthem's opening motif, an ascending octave leap on the words "Come all," summons the citizenry to action, while the quick-paced measures that follow (the verse) illustrate the urgency of the situation through a rallying text declaimed to a plethora of dotted rhythms and triplets. The haunting march refrain, marked "not too fast," is set apart through its minor mode and distinctive rhythmic elements. This choice of mode on Friml's part is extremely unusual, for most populist marches are in a major key. Perhaps Friml chose the minor mode to give the song a sense of historical distance, equating the minor mode with the past. Regardless, the modal shift between verse and refrain adds dramatic impetus to the opening phrase of the AABA refrain. Friml added further individuality to the A sections of the song through a skilled use of metric anticipation ("Sons of **toil** and danger") and accented repeated notes ("**And bow down** to Burgundy") in which certain words of the text are emphasized through musical means. This is especially evident in the final A section, where the lyrics assert self-determination: the metrically anticipated "Sons of **France** around us" and the thrice accented "**And to Hell** with Burgundy!"

Villon introduces the song as he enters the Fir Cone Tavern, singing its verse and refrain. The full chorus—not just a male chorus—immediately repeats the refrain. This is not a male choral march, as was "The Mounties" in *Rose Marie*, but involves everyone onstage joining in the fight against tyranny.

"Song of the Vagabonds" returns throughout the show as an aural indicator of both Villon and the strength of the people. Villon's followers sing it as they leave to fight Burgundy in act 3 and during their triumphant return in act 4. It also appears as underscoring at key points in the drama: in the act 1 finale when Villon insults the king, during Louis's monologue at the beginning of act 2 when the monarch is bemoaning Villon's disparaging remarks, at the end of act 2 when the Herald of Burgundy arrives and challenges the grand marshall (Villon in disguise) to battle, during the act 3 entr'acte (orchestral introduction) that establishes the strength lying beneath the surface of the masque, and late in act 3 as Villon plans his attack on the Burgundian troops with his men, not the king's.

Creating what became such an important anthem against oppression posed a formidable challenge to Friml. As he recalled, "And that damn 'song to save France.' I composed a dozen melodies. Janney listened and shook his head. I remember he said, 'It's got to *roar*! It's got to have humor! It's got to sweep America—as it is supposed to sweep all France in our story!' How the heck could a song both *roar* and *have humor*? And who would give a wooden nickel anyway for a song that he wanted the tag line to be 'And to hell with Burgundy'!"[19]

As was typical for Friml, inspiration arrived in the middle of the night. The first six notes, "Sons of toil and danger," were born at the piano in the presence of Janney and Hooker, and the rest of the melody arrived within ten minutes. Friml handed the music to Hooker, who stayed up the rest of the night writing the lyric.[20]

Community is an important dimension of *The Vagabond King*, reflected musically not just in "Song of the Vagabonds" but also in the other ensemble numbers, including act 1's opening chorus and the "Nocturne" at the beginning of act 3. In order to establish act 1's setting as a tavern, Friml and his collaborators decided that a drinking song was the most appropriate means for doing so. The song comes on the heels of Romberg's highly successful "Drinking Song" in *The Student Prince*, itself part of a tradition of Broadway drinking songs that includes "Brown October Ale" in Reginald De Koven's *Robin Hood* (1891). But *The Vagabond King*'s opening number is no ordinary Bacchan ode, for its text is in two languages, English and Latin. The song begins with gendered divisions: the women (the prostitutes) sing in English ("Life is like a bubble in our glasses"), while the men (the students) sing in Latin ("In taberna gaudeat ebrius mero!" [In the tavern we gather and make merry]). Soon, everyone sings together in either English or Latin as an expression of their shared camaraderie.

By contrast, the choral "Nocturne" establishes a quiet atmosphere at the beginning of the masque. Its opening lyric, "In the night, while the winds are murmuring low," along with its gently rollicking musical style, recall "Oh, dry the glist'ning tear" and "Sighing softly to the river" from act 2 of Gilbert and Sullivan's *The Pirates of Penzance* (1880).

The male chorus, which in 1920s operetta became associated with heroism and camaraderie, takes on an opposite function in *The Vagabond King*, providing comic relief as Louis's Scotch Archers. In "Scotch Archers' Song," they describe their job at the gallows, with spoken "woof"s signifying the moment the victims fall in their nooses. Literal laughing syllables ("ha, ha, ha") and lyrics describing an executionee as "dancing on the balmy breezes, in her little white chemises" contribute to the overall image of the guard as being less than noble. Its sluggardly moderate tempo and general carefree spirit distinguish it from the heroic "Song of the Vagabonds." The king's archers are not concerned about social justice, unlike Villon's followers.

Huguette is among the most memorable of any female operetta character. This "Daughter of Carmen" bears a stronger resemblance to her ancestor than does Wanda in *Rose Marie*. Huguette and Carmen love passionately, dance in taverns, and die onstage. Huguette, however, is deeply devoted to one man, Villon. Early in act 1, she reads a poem Villon wrote for her and her colleagues, whom he calls "daughters of pleasure." This becomes the verse of "Love for Sale," in which Huguette describes her profession. Friml's descending melodic lines and fluctuating tempos amplify the sultriness and ultimate melancholy of the lyric. As was the case with "Why Shouldn't We?" in *Rose Marie*, this song also anticipates one by Cole Porter: "Love for Sale" from *The New Yorkers* (1930), another song in which a prostitute explains her vocation.

In act 3, Huguette denies Noel's sexual advances in the poignant "Huguette's Waltz." Through powerful lyrics such as "Never try to bind me" and "Love and let me go!," Huguette shows herself to be Carmen's progeny. Neither woman wants to be captured and kept.

During the operetta's genesis, Janney told Friml that he wanted a great waltz for Huguette. Friml responded, "A waltz is just going up and down the scale," and proceeded to play a descending scale at the piano as a joke. This evolved into the highly chromatic and melancholic melody of "Huguette's Waltz."[21] The descending chromaticism of the tune provides another tie to Carmen, whose "Habanera" has a similar melodic shape.

Both of Huguette's songs are reprised as orchestral underscoring later in the show. The most poignant instance is that of "Love for Sale," which is played as Huguette dies in Villon's arms. Twenty-first-century audiences surely see this scene through the lens of "A Little Fall of Rain," the song in which Eponine dies in Marius's arms in Schönberg and Boublil's musical version of *Les Misérables*.

Katherine and Villon, the romantic leads, sing the score's most luscious music; their songs, like those of Rose Marie and Jim in *Rose Marie*, are what, in musical terms, distinguishes this show as an operetta. Katherine's "Some Day," the song she sings to Villon's words, is a lyrical, expressive ballad filled with distinctive falling thirds. Consisting only of a refrain in ABAC form, the number requires tremendous vocal control and an extensive range. As with most of the songs in *The Vagabond King*, this one is reprised at key moments, including a choral version in the act 2 finale and then as underscoring in the final scene when Katherine saves her lover from the gallows.

"Only a Rose" is the principal recurring love duet, endorsing the physical symbol of the rose that represents Katherine and Villon's love. Its opening words, "Red rose—out of the east," are set to a minor mode melody with a relatively static harmony, and a waft of Orientalist exoticism enters the sound palette. The same melody is repeated, however, for "Red rose—out of the west," ending the Orientalist text-music relationship. The refrain itself, one of Friml's most famous ballads, is in the same form as "Some Day" (ABAC), indicating a textual-musical relationship between the two songs as expressions of the underlying love between Katherine and Villon. The refrain returns as the basis for the act 4 finale, in which the chorus joins the romantic leads in the confession of their love.

The rapturous waltz duet "Love Me Tonight" is another of the score's highlights. Not until the end of the song do Katherine and Villon sing the same music. Friml's fine contrapuntal skills as well as his effective use of chromatic harmony are evident throughout the emotive number in which the protagonists start in different places, singing their own music, and end up together, paralleling their actions in the story.

"Love Me Tonight" is one of three waltzes in act 3, the other two being "Serenade" and "Huguette's Waltz." "Serenade" is a comic number during which Tabarie and Oliver compete for Lady Mary's affection. Its decidedly lighthearted character is increased by the occasional appearance of the words "plim plim," imitating a lute, on beats two and three. These three waltzes accentuate different dimensions of the show's narrative: humor in "Serenade," tragedy in "Huguette's Waltz," and romance in "Love Me Tonight." Friml thus employed the same musical idiom to serve three different functions. Waltzes do not have to be love songs, nor, as in the instances of "Some Day" and "Only a Rose," do love songs have to be waltzes. Friml thus successfully challenged the operetta trope of love songs being equated with triple meter.

Medieval Themes and *The Vagabond King*

As a tale set in fifteenth-century Paris, *The Vagabond King*'s incorporation of medieval symbolism, historically accurate depictions, and characters drawn from Villon's own writings give the show a level of credibility not usually associated with the Broadway musical. Hooker, with his academic background, no doubt was responsible for this historicity. These elements follow the tenets of Villon's own writings, where he provided detailed vignettes in addition to a grand, sweeping narrative.

The dominant medieval symbol in *The Vagabond King* is the rose, epitomized in the song "Only a Rose." During the Middle Ages, the rose was considered the "Queen of Flowers," a symbol of the Virgin Mary, and a representation of romance.[22] The rose symbolized both religious devotion and human love. These two meanings infuse *The Vagabond King*: Villon mentions that his first view of Katherine was as she was praying, and Katherine brings a rose to the Fir Cone Tavern, a profane venue, to give to her lover. Roses were also known for their ability to purify: Katherine, by giving Villon a rose, could instigate his moral redemption. The red rose, the first image in the verse of "Only a Rose," is, because of its color, associated with martyrdom. In *The Vagabond King*, Villon and his followers are willing to sacrifice their lives for France.

Katherine is posited as a Marian figure in act 2, for in the Middle Ages, a maiden in a garden was one symbolic depiction of the Virgin. This becomes significant in the context of Saint Bernard's comparisons of the Virgin's charity to a red rose and her virginity to a white one. Both colors are mentioned in Hooker's lyrics for "Only a Rose." Katherine demonstrates these qualities, for she is generous, saving Villon from the gallows, and also pure, saving herself for him.

Beyond evoking medieval symbolism, the creators' concern for historical accuracy is immediately evident in the first scene at the Fir Cone Tavern. The tavern's name is a direct reference to Dionysus, the Greek god of wine, for Dionysus's rod, the thyrsus, had a fir cone at its tip. (Classical antiquity was important in medieval culture and learning.) It was normal in the Middle Ages for women to run taverns, which is the situation in *The Vagabond King* with Margot being the proprietress. The venue's physical arrangement, with a downstairs tavern and upstairs brothel, is likewise historically accurate. Additionally, the notion of being "King for a Day" came from an established medieval Carnival tradition. During the upside-down, topsy-turvy pre-Lenten celebrations, it was not uncommon for the village fool to become "King for a Day"; here, it was the "King of the Vagabonds" who fulfilled this role.

Villon's autobiographical *Testament* includes real-life inspirations for two prominent characters in *The Vagabond King*: Katherine and Thibaut. In the poem, Villon mentions a woman by the name of Katherine Vausselles with whom he had an "amorous misadventure." Nothing specific is known about her, but there was a Vaucelles family residing in the neighborhood where Villon grew up. The historical Thibaut was a bishop, and Villon spent the summer of 1461 in his prison.[23] The two men had known each other in real life, and their enmity was transferred to the Broadway stage.

Political Resonances

Villon was a student, and for audiences in 1925, the notion of student-led uprisings in France echoed events of 1832 and 1848. French student rebellions were a known quantity. The 1832 revolution was the one immortalized by Victor Hugo in his novel *Les Misérables* (1862), a work known to the creators of *The Vagabond King*. A subplot about students taking up arms against corruption and injustice and willing to die for their cause occurs in both stories.

In *The Vagabond King*, Paris is surrounded, this time by Burgundians, who, for the 1920s audience, were foils for the Germans. To Francophile audiences who saw *The Vagabond King*, there was an immediate association between the surrounding of Paris in the fifteenth century and its siege during World War I. "To Hell with Burgundy" meant "To Hell with Germany, Communism, Fascism, and any other regime that abuses human freedom."

These political sentiments regarding political freedom had continued autobiographical resonances for Friml. First, he became a naturalized U.S. citizen in 1925, the very year in which *The Vagabond King* appeared.[24] Second, after World War II and the Communist takeover of Czechoslovakia, his homeland was stripped of freedom. He wrote to President Lyndon B. Johnson in 1968: "Today, my native land is locked in the vice of International Communism and suppression. My heart goes out to those former countrymen who have never known the freedom afforded in the United States. It is because I have seen both sides of the coin that I understand why America—the United States—must continue to lead the world toward freedom in the face of organized enslavement within the confines of that hatred, and I hope rusting, iron curtain."[25] Friml and Villon shared a vision of freedom from political oppression. Perhaps this is why, when pushed on the subject, Friml privileged *The Vagabond King* as his favorite show.

Screen Versions of *The Vagabond King*

François Villon's tale, as depicted in the play *If I Were King*, has a strong film legacy. Nonmusical versions include the silent *The Beloved Rogue* (1927), featuring John Barrymore in one of his finest performances, and *If I Were King* (1938), a highly literate interpretation that starred Ronald Colman as François, Basil Rathbone as King Louis XI, and Frances Dee as Katherine. But it is the two film versions of Friml's musicalized version that concern us here. Both were Paramount Studios releases: the first, in 1930, starred Dennis King and Jeanette MacDonald, while the second, from 1956, featured Kathryn Grayson and Oreste Kirkop, a then (and unfortunately now) virtually unknown singer.

The 1930 film of *The Vagabond King* strove to demonstrate the various aesthetic possibilities inherent in the film medium. In some ways, it surpassed these intentions, becoming overly pretentious in its literary, painterly, and musical qualities.[26] But these ostentations certainly resulted in a lavish cinematic spectacle. Its stars were stage veteran King, who was still enjoying fame for creating the title role in *The Vagabond King*'s Broadway production and also appearing as d'Artagnan in Friml's *The Three Musketeers* (to be discussed in the next chapter). Jeanette MacDonald, on the other hand, was a newcomer to Hollywood, for this was only her second film, the first being the previous year's *The Love Parade*.

As was necessary for the film medium, several aspects of the story were altered. Although the film opens in the tavern with Villon reading poems about Louis's ineffectiveness, it quickly moves to the church where Villon spies Katherine and joins her in prayer at the altar. She gives him a gold coin as she leaves, thinking him a beggar. After Villon protects Katherine by driving back her would-be abductors (sent there under orders from the grand marshall), she responds by pledging that she will love the man who fights off the Burgundians. Katherine returns to her lodgings, and offscreen, in her chamber, begins to sing "Some Day." Villon hears the disembodied voice and is drawn to her window. During the orchestral coda, she goes out on her balcony as Villon reaches his hand toward her. She does not see it, so she reenters her room and goes to bed. Immediately, Villon begins his wishful ballad, "If I Were King," newly written for the film by Sam Coslow, Newell Chase, and Leo Robin.[27]

At the "Tavern of the Vagabonds" (no longer the Fir Cone Tavern), the king and Tristan arrive incognito and the narrative continues as in the stage version, with the notable omission of Katherine's arrival and the song "Only a Rose." After Villon accepts the king's offer to rule for seven days (as opposed to twenty-four hours), the king's servants, in a manic routine to frantic music, transform Villon into the Count of Montcorbier, the new grand marshall.

The scene shifts to the rose garden, where "Only a Rose" is playing as underscoring. Katherine enters, introduces herself to the grand marshall, and asks him to save Villon's life. She then informs Montcorbier that only he who will save France can gain her favor and gives him a rose as a symbol of her promise. Katherine and Villon sing "Only a Rose" as an expression of their mutual pact.

The Burgundian Herald arrives, as in the stage version, followed by Huguette's waltz (now called "The Vagabond King Waltz," indicating the prostitute's diminished role in the film) and Villon and Katherine's "Love Me Tonight."[28] Huguette dies in her true love's arms, and Villon and his followers defeat the Burgundians. In a detail not in the stage libretto but in McCarthy's story, Louis calls for an inch of candle to be brought from the church. Villon will die unless someone offers to take his place before the candle burns out. The film ends with Katherine saving Villon's life and the two of them leading the chorus in a reprise of "Only a Rose" (as in the stage version).

The tale's fundamental focus is shifted in the film from social responsibility (although Katherine says she will only love a man who will save France) to its leads, both the characters and the actors who played them. The first musical numbers in the film are Katherine's "Some Day" and Villon's "If I Were King" sung in immediate succession. MacDonald and King thus each have a solo number within the film's opening minutes. The rowdy choral numbers with students and prostitutes give way to luxurious romance and noble dreaming.

One of the film's most impressive sequences is the battle between Villon's troops and the Burgundians. Filmed as a night march, the male chorus (as opposed to a mixed one) sings "Song of the Vagabonds" against non-synchronized trumpet calls. A superimposed cameo of MacDonald's face and flowing orange hair (in the two-color Technicolor version) glistens on-screen, inspiring Villon to victory.[29] The Parisians are in church, with a choir singing a "Miserere," when the victorious vagabonds return to the strains of their song. Diegetic bells and organ, neither of which are synchronized with the "Miserere" or the "Song of the Vagabonds," create a complex polyphonic sound web. Those in the church would actually be listening to the "Miserere," while those in the streets would heed the "Song of the Vagabonds." Everyone would experience the bells, while only some would be aware of the trumpet calls and the organ.

Although producers adored King, MacDonald expressed annoyance at her costar, who not only held tremendous backstage sway but also enjoyed stealing scenes.[30] One famous anecdote relates to the filming of "Only a Rose." The scene was planned so that MacDonald would be alone on-screen, save for one brief reaction shot of King, until the concluding duet. But the attention-seeking actor, despite having a hobbyhorse placed in front of him, managed to insert his fingers, nose, and pompadour into the frame. The shot went uncorrected, causing great consternation (very understandably) for MacDonald. She subsequently referred to the song as "Only a Nose."[31]

The 1956 film version starred Kathryn Grayson and "new singing sensation" Oreste Kirkop, a tenor from Malta who used only his first name in Hollywood but never made anymore Hollywood musicals after *The Vagabond King.* The legendary Michael Curtiz directed the film; among Curtiz's many other credits are *The Adventures of Robin Hood* (1938), *Angels with Dirty Faces* (1938), *The Private*

Dennis King and Jeanette MacDonald in the 1930 film version of The Vagabond King. *Hulton Archive, Margaret Chute / Getty Images.*

Lives of Elizabeth & Essex (1939), *The Sea Hawk* (1940), *Casablanca* (1942), *Yankee Doodle Dandy* (1942), *Mildred Pierce* (1945), and *White Christmas* (1954). Several recognizable actors had supporting roles, including Rita Moreno (Huguette), Leslie Nielsen (Thibault, whose name is spelled differently in the film version), Phyllis Newman (Lulu), and—heard but not seen—Vincent Price (narrator). Its team, both in front of and behind the camera, was formidable.

The film blends aspects of Errol Flynn's *The Adventures of Robin Hood,* also set in the Middle Ages, with MGM's film version of *Kiss Me, Kate* (1953). This *Vagabond King* bears an uncanny resemblance to *Kiss Me, Kate* in terms of costuming, choreography, sets, and, in many ways, music. Kathryn Grayson starred in both films, after all, and she possessed a name that would draw audiences to the cinema. Especially considering that no one had heard of Oreste, it was imperative to have a recognizable name on the marquee. Unfortunately, the film arrived at a time when big-budget, lavishly produced film musicals were on the decline. They were expensive to make, and audience interest in the genre was waning.

Only four songs, "Some Day," "Huguette's Waltz," "Only a Rose," and "Song of the Vagabonds," came from the original stage version. (How wonderful it would have been to hear Grayson and Oreste sing "Love Me Tonight.") Friml wrote five new songs with lyricist Johnny Burke for the film: "Bon Jour," "Comparisons," "This Same Heart," "Vive la You," and "Watch Out for the Devil." The first three were written especially for Oreste, while the other two are lavish production numbers. Significantly, the new songs outnumber the old ones in the film—this was a Paramount Studios film musical, not a Broadway operetta.

The three songs for Oreste each showcase a different aspect of the star's vocal and acting abilities. "Bon Jour," as the film's first musical number, introduces Oreste as a singing actor and Villon as a populist-rooted character. The boisterous affirming anthem, which Villon sings atop a cart while driving through the countryside into the city, gave Oreste plenty of opportunity to showcase his winning smile, gregarious screen presence, good looks, and high tenor register. "Comparisons," by contrast, is a humorous solo madrigal filled with hee-haws and other animal sounds. Perhaps Friml was thinking of the onomatopoetic chansons of Clément Janequin (ca. 1485–1558) such as "Le Chant des Oiseaux" (The Song of the Birds), for "Comparisons" is filled with animal references, including one that stated that France would be all right if the king were as bright as a donkey or a crow. In this song, the film's creators, unlike those of the stage version, conflated the Middle Ages and the Renaissance. Oreste's third song, "This Same Heart," a romantic ballad, radiates lyricism and is one of the film's musical highlights.

"Vive la You," the first song sung in the tavern, is a sanitized version of "Danse bohème" from *Carmen* and replaced the morally ambiguous "Love for Sale." Like "Love for Sale," "Vive la You" features Huguette, played here by Rita Moreno. The fast-paced dance number is filled with energy and plenty of toasts to wine. It has a slight Latin tinge in which Moreno foreshadows her future role as Anita in the film version of *West Side Story* (1961).

"Watch Out for the Devil" is the diegetic number performed at the masque. Villon and Catherine (spelled in the film with a *C*) sing the lyrics offstage but on-screen. It closely resembles "From This Moment On" from *Kiss Me, Kate* in its length (five and a half minutes) and choreographic spectacle.

The Vagabond King, like its immediate predecessor, *Rose Marie*, enjoyed tremendous success onstage. The film versions of *The Vagabond King*, however, did not achieve the same level of popularity as those of *Rose Marie*. The 1936 version of *Rose Marie* benefited from being a star vehicle for the established team of Jeanette MacDonald and Nelson Eddy, and its 1954 version took advantage of stunning scenery. *The Vagabond King* did not enjoy such luxuries, for the 1930 version appeared when film musicals were still a relatively new medium, and the 1956 version was released just as interest in lavishly costumed musical films was diminishing and giving way to more realistic approaches to the genre.

5 | The Challenge
of Success

WITH TWO HITS IN a row, *Rose Marie* and *The Vagabond King*, Rudolf Friml's reputation was established. Now the acclaimed Broadway composer found himself facing a daunting professional challenge: having to maintain the extraordinary level of his previous accomplishments.

Producer Arthur Hammerstein wanted the creative team of *Rose Marie* (Friml, Otto Harbach, Herbert Stothart, and Oscar Hammerstein 2nd) to work together again, this time on *Song of the Flame* (December 30, 1925, 44th Street Theatre), a romantic operetta set in pre-Revolutionary Russia with a finale that takes place in post–World War I Paris. Friml turned down the offer because he would have had to work alongside Herbert Stothart.[1] George Gershwin took Friml's place on the project, resulting in the only musical on which Gershwin and Hammerstein collaborated.

By late 1925, Friml had developed a distinctive and identifiable musical theater style. At its center were sweeping love songs for the romantic leads, both of whom had to have classically trained voices. Orbiting these songs, which could be either waltzes or ballads, were grand choral marches and humorous numbers, usually for secondary characters, that were characterized by dotted rhythms and syncopations. Glimpses at musical exoticism, such as the Orientalist tinge in *Katinka*'s "Allah's Holiday" and the Indianist tropes in *Rose Marie*, were also part of the palette. From a musical-dramatic perspective, characters were defined through their music—songs were not interchangeable, as they could be in a revue or even in many musical comedies. Finally, the use of carefully selected underscoring took on increased significance; for example, "Wanda's Theme" plays during the scene in which Wanda murders her husband in *Rose Marie*, and "Love for Sale" accompanies Huguette's death in *The Vagabond King*.

It was not just Friml who was emerging as a leader of American operetta during the 1920s but also Sigmund Romberg.[2] Romberg's sentimental approach to operetta, which he developed with the Shuberts, culminated in *The Student Prince*. Here, as in previous successes such as *Maytime*, the story ends with the principals not being together, and the score is unified musically through a recurring waltz. A new approach to the genre emerged in Romberg's two other especially significant operettas from the decade, *The Desert Song* and *The New Moon*. Happy endings became the norm, nostalgia was minimized, recurring primary love duets no longer were exclusively waltzes, and male choruses sang marches with socially relevant lyrics. These elements exist in *Rose Marie* and *The Vagabond King*, and these shows surely must have influenced Romberg. Rudimentary musical exoticism is also featured in Romberg's works from the later 1920s, for in *The Desert Song*, Arab characters sing in minor and French ones in major, and a sultry tango, "Softly, as in a Morning Sunrise," is one of the musical highpoints of *The New Moon*. As it had been in the previous decade, Friml's harmonic language remained more chromatic than that of Romberg's, while Romberg tended to create more extended musical-dramatic scenes than his Czech-born contemporary.

Friml and Romberg had a great deal in common, for they both worked on Broadway in the 1920s and both moved to Hollywood in the 1930s. When asked in an interview if he knew Romberg, Friml responded, "Very well, very well. . . . [W]e were good friends. I drank a lot of beer with him."[3]

None of Friml's Broadway works from *Rose Marie* on were actually called operettas on their playbills, but all were referred to as such by critics and among the general public. Each was labeled a "musical play," except for *Luana* (1930), which was a "Musical Romance (Play) of the South Seas," and *Music Hath Charms* (1934), described as "A Play with Music." These appellations, all of which include the root words "music" and "play," carry several implications. First, the term "operetta" was problematic in the years following World War I because of its Germanic associations—Broadway was a commercial enterprise, and producers needed to be sensitive to the anti-German feeling that lingered after the war ended. Second, by using permutations of the words "play" and "music," creators were demonstrating an intentional integration of drama and song. These works were not exclusively operettas, musical comedies, or revues, according to the genres' earlier definitions, but rather incorporated and combined various musical styles according to the particular dictates of the story.

Two Failures: *The Wild Rose* and *The White Eagle*

The pair of Friml shows that followed the immensely successful *Rose Marie* and *The Vagabond King* did not continue his trend of successes: *The Wild Rose* (October 20, 1926, Martin Beck Theatre) was performed only sixty-one times, *The White Eagle* (December 26, 1927, Casino Theatre) only forty-eight. Both shows incorporated elements from their two immediate predecessors, but those attempts actually did more to hurt the new shows than help them. Audiences saw the devices for what they were: imitations.

The plot of *The Wild Rose* concerns American Monty Travers, whose winnings in Monte Carlo help Princess Elise of Borovina (a Ruritanian principality) outwit malevolent oil promoters and Bolshevists. Ever the hero, he even thwarts a bomb intended for the Borovinian king. Like *The Vagabond King*, this show included a prominent theme of social responsibility and boasted a heroic male choral march, "Lady of the Rose," which was in the same vein as "Song of the Vagabonds." The score also offered the romantic duet "One Golden Hour" and folk dances from the fictional Slavic Borovina. The dances gave the show an ethnic flair, recalling "Totem Tom-Tom" in *Rose Marie* and its extended dance sequence, but in reality harkened back even further to Franz Lehár and his Pontevedrian music for 1905's *Die lustige Witwe*.

Oscar Hammerstein 2nd and Otto Harbach signed contracts to co-write the book and lyrics for both *The Wild Rose* and *The Desert Song*. The collaborators decided to share the credit but to divide the work. Harbach would work with Friml and Hammerstein with Romberg. *The Wild Rose* underwent many changes during its tryout to the point that very few of Hammerstein's ideas remained in the show, even though he was credited with book and lyrics.[4] Hammerstein's project, *The Desert Song*, fared much better than Harbach's, for it played 471 performances, was filmed three times in full-length versions, and remains part of the operetta repertory.

The second show, *The White Eagle*, should have been a success, for its plot included Native Americans, following on the popularity of *Rose Marie*, and its creative team was the same as that of *The Vagabond King*: producer Russell Janney, composer Rudolf Friml, and librettists and lyricists W. H. Post and Brian

Hooker. *The White Eagle*'s failure cannot be blamed entirely on the show itself, for it had the misfortune to open the night before the epochal *Show Boat* (music by Jerome Kern, book and lyrics by Oscar Hammerstein 2nd) had its New York premiere at the Ziegfeld Theatre. Theatrical attention focused on that show and not on *The White Eagle*.

A musical version of Edwin Milton Royle's highly successful play *The Squaw Man* (1905), *The White Eagle* faithfully followed its source material. James, brother of the Earl of Kerhill, takes the blame for a dishonorable action by the earl and flees to the American West. As Jim Carson, he becomes a successful rancher and marries Silverwing, a Native American woman, with whom he has a son, Hal. When the earl dies childless back in England, Jim is set to inherit his title, but Silverwing, believing that her presence will hinder the futures of her husband and son, kills herself.

The show failed to impress critics. J. Brooks Atkinson wrote, in his *New York Times* review,

> The resulting operetta, called "The White Eagle," combined the best and worst features of an effort to get the most out of poor old Puccini, Gilbert & Sullivan and the conventional Broadway musical show. There was a little bit of everything and too much of some things.
>
> The effect was a sort of musical cafeteria where one might take one's choice. There was a good song in every act, there were marvelously effective stage settings and costumes—designed by James Reynolds—and some bizarre and original choreographic work.[5]

A heroine who commits suicide (in the manner of Puccini's *Madama Butterfly* [1904]) and an Englishman concerned about honor (typical of Gilbert and Sullivan) are the unlikely romantic leads. Friml's eclectic approach to the score—one of the reasons *Rose Marie* and *The Vagabond King* work so well—did not please Atkinson. Neither did the choreography of Busby Berkeley, the visionary whose geometric designs and innovative camera angles helped define early musical film choreography. If Berkeley's efforts for *The White Eagle* were in any way indicative of what he would do on-screen in the 1930s, it is no wonder that Atkinson found the choreography "bizarre."

Although its creative team was that of *The Vagabond King* and the new musical even opened at the same theater as its successful predecessor (the Casino, incidentally the house where Romberg's *The Desert Song* also played), *The White Eagle* is much closer in concept and execution to *Rose Marie*. It seems as if the creators of *The Vagabond King* were trying to capitalize on the popularity of *Rose Marie* as opposed to that of their own show.

The Indianist elements constitute the most obvious parallels with *Rose Marie*.

Friml created a Native American sound world in *The White Eagle* with the same fundamental tropes he used in the earlier show. This is apparent in a dream ballet (predating the one in *Oklahoma!* by sixteen years) and also in act 3's "Dance, Dance, Dance," a direct descendent of *Rose Marie*'s "Totem Tom-Tom." But the song with the closest links to *Rose Marie* in both dramatic function and musical style is Silverwing's "Alone."

Silverwing confesses that she will sing "Alone" only to the man she will marry, following Rose Marie's pledge regarding "Indian Love Call." Furthermore, "Alone" is reprised throughout the operetta as an aural symbol of the love between Silverwing and Jim, again recalling the treatment of "Indian Love Call." The lyrics of Silverwing's song allude directly to its ancestor through the emphatic repetition of the words "calling you," the final two words of the opening phrase of the refrain of "Indian Love Call," "When I'm calling you." Musically, the song endorses several Indianist tropes, including repeated bass notes, open fifths in the accompaniment, and chromatic obbligato flourishes. The song's most distinguishing feature, though, is its prominence of ascending thirds, not an Indianist identifier, but an important feature nonetheless.

In act 3, Silverwing sings "Indian Lullaby" to her son. Its melody, like that of "Alone," is filled with ascending thirds, which forms a connection between the two songs. The rising third interval functions here as a leitmotif—a recurring aural indicator—for Silverwing's love. The heroine expresses her love through rising thirds, first for Jim in "Alone" and then for Hal in "Indian Lullaby."

The White Eagle has a heroic march for male chorus, following the precedent of "The Mounties" in *Rose Marie*. But rather than endorsing the Royal Canadian Mounted Police, "Regimental Song" extols the merits of British imperial regiments around the world and features geographic-specific lyrics such as "north of Labrador," "south of Singapore," and "east of Mandalay." Jim, the romantic lead, sings two fine ballads, "Give Me One Hour" and "A Home for You." Both exude broad lyricism, and "Give Me One Hour," with its soaring melody, enjoyed its own popularity outside of the show.[6]

After two failures, Friml was understandably hoping for a hit with his next show, *The Three Musketeers*. The heroic storyline, implicit romance, and opportunity to work again with leading man Dennis King certainly appealed to him. Furthermore, Florenz Ziegfeld, with whom he had worked on two editions of the *Follies* in the early 1920s, was going to produce the show. The ingredients for success were present, as they had been for *The White Eagle*, but this time the result was a triumph.

Return to Success: *The Three Musketeers*

Alexandre Dumas's novel *The Three Musketeers* (1844) attracted the attention of
Ziegfeld, who brought his experience from mounting *Show Boat* as well as the
lavish and splendor-filled series of *Follies* to his spectacular musical version of
the novel. William Anthony McGuire crafted the book, while Clifford Grey and
P. G. Wodehouse shared responsibility for the lyrics. Joseph Urban designed the
opulent sets, and his work as set designer for Ziegfeld's *Follies* was evident in the
spaciousness of the decor. Albertina Rasch, one of the first dance directors to be
called a "choreographer," created the dances, infusing them with ballet elements
that accentuated the show's courtly atmosphere.

The expanse of Dumas's original book needed to be abridged for a musical
treatment. McGuire, therefore, included only three episodes in his libretto, all of
which center on d'Artagnan: his first meeting with Athos, Porthos, and Aramis;
his romance with Constance Bonacieux; and his trip to England to retrieve the
queen's jewels from the Duke of Buckingham, to whom she had given them. Rev-
eling in his glory as François Villon in *The Vagabond King* (and still remembered
for creating Jim in *Rose Marie*), Dennis King played the lead role of d'Artagnan.
New York Times reviewer J. Brooks Atkinson wrote that Ziegfeld's choice to cast
King "very nearly measures his perfection."[7] Vivienne Segal, fresh from her lau-
rels as Margot in Romberg's *The Desert Song*, was Constance.

The Three Musketeers opened on March 13, 1928, at the Lyric Theatre to tremendous critical acclaim. Atkinson heralded the "rushing, captivating score by
Rudolf Friml."[8] In another *New York Times* article, he wrote: "Excepting Jerome
Kern's genuine creative musical score for 'Show Boat,' Rudolf Friml's compositions for 'The Three Musketeers' are the best in the current Ziegfeld productions. Something of the purple fury of the Dumas romance colors Mr. Friml's
solid score straight through from the overture."[9]

Friml's outstanding numbers for *The Three Musketeers* include rousing male
choral marches, soaring ballads, a love waltz, and a sentimental semicomic song,
all of which fit into a general lyrical operetta style. Musical comedy numbers are
notably absent, making the score for *The Three Musketeers*, because of the nature
of the story, the most homogeneous in Friml's output. This stylistic unity most
likely accounts for why Atkinson, in his *New York Times* reviews, praised the score
of *The Three Musketeers* and censured that of *The White Eagle*.

Heroic marches in *The Three Musketeers* continue the legacy of "The Mounties" and "Song of the Vagabonds." "All for One and One for All" is the second
song in the operetta (following the opening chorus "Summer Time," sung by the

villagers) and the one in which we meet the legendary Musketeers. D'Artagnan, as the operetta's hero, leads the next march, "My Sword (and I)," in which he describes the fear his sword inspires. The song's minor mode creates a fundamental sense of foreboding and trepidation and also gives both the song and the sword it describes a mythical quality.

The verse of the show's third march, "March of the Musketeers," which affirms the legion's legendary status, is in the minor mode. This feature connects it not only to "My Sword (and I)" but also to previous Friml marches, namely the opening of "The Mounties" and the refrain of "Song of the Vagabonds," which are also in minor. The verse also recalls that of "Song of the Vagabonds" with its array of dotted rhythms. In the major-mode refrain, the reality of the Musketeers' heroism is brought to the fore, paralleling what Friml did in "The Mounties." This modal change accentuates the lyrics, which shift from describing the Musketeers' reputation (verse) to their reality (refrain). This march and "My Sword (and I)" are reprised throughout the show as aural symbols of d'Artagnan and the Musketeers.

With its connections to earlier marches, "March of the Musketeers" represents a synthesis of Friml's approaches to heroic operetta marches. The minor mode is favored, especially when lyrics concern either fear and trepidation or legendary reputations. But the major mode is also present in order to root the songs

The Three Musketeers face d'Artagnan (Dennis King) in the original production of The Three Musketeers. *Culver Pictures, Inc.*

in the present-tense contexts of their respective storylines. Heroism prevails, as Friml asserts through the major mode.

The show's outstanding ballad is the languid "Ma Belle." Although originally sung by Aramis leading the chorus, it has sometimes been reassigned to d'Artagnan, as on the *Railroad Hour* radio broadcast with Gordon MacRae that aired on January 28, 1952. Other fine ballads include the queen's lyrical "My Dreams," Buckingham's expansive "Queen of My Heart," and Constance's graceful "Ev'ry Little While."

"Your Eyes" is a sweeping waltz in which d'Artagnan and Constance confess their fidelity, even though they must part.[10] It follows the precedents of the prominent waltzes "Door of My Dreams" in *Rose Marie* and "Love Me Tonight" in *The Vagabond King* and, like those waltzes, is not reprised later in the show.

In Constance's lighthearted "He for Me," the heroine describes her ideal man while each of the Three Musketeers tells her how he fits the bill. A duple-meter number in moderate tempo, it foreshadows Guenevere and the knights' "Then You May Take Me to the Fair" from Alan Jay Lerner and Frederick Loewe's *Camelot* (1960) in both dramatic content and general musical style.

The Three Musketeers was a solid hit with its 318 performances, though not as strong as either *Rose Marie* or *The Vagabond King*. The musical also played in London, with Dennis King reprising the lead role, at the Theatre Royal, Drury Lane, where it opened on March 28, 1930, for a respectable run of 240 performances.

In the film *The Great Ziegfeld* (1936), *The Three Musketeers* appears in the montage "Four Hits in a Season," alongside *Rio Rita*, *Whoopee*, and *Show Boat*. Instrumental motifs from the first three titles are heard in the background, followed by the end of the refrain of *Show Boat*'s "Ol' Man River." Four measures of "March of the Musketeers" represent *The Three Musketeers*. The march also appears in the death montage at the end of the film.

Curiously, although various versions and reinterpretations of the Dumas tale have been filmed, no screen versions of Friml's operetta were ever made. Douglas Fairbanks (1921), John Wayne (1933), Richard Chamberlain (1974), and Charlie Sheen (1993) are among the actors who have brought d'Artagnan to life on-screen. Why have not any singing actors done so?

Two More Flops and the End of a Broadway Career

Friml composed only two more operettas after *The Three Musketeers*: *Luana* and *Music Hath Charms*. Unfortunately, both were failures and colored the end of Friml's important and impressive Broadway career. With the financial security garnered from his nearly two decades as a leading Broadway composer, the failures hurt Friml's ego more than his bank account.

While the overall quality of the two creations may have been partly to blame for their closures, one also has to consider economics. With the stock market crash in 1929 and subsequent Great Depression, the Broadway industry suffered terribly. Theaters closed, bankruptcies were common, and production costs had to be cut substantially wherever and whenever possible. These factors certainly made it difficult to mount lavish spectacles featuring large choruses. Producers had to be careful in what they attempted to put onstage. Operettas were expensive propositions, and few producers were willing to mount them. When they did, they were taking a tremendous financial risk.

Luana (September 17, 1930, Hammerstein's Theatre) was originally going to be a film musical, but when the Hollywood project folded, it was revised for the stage. Friml worked with two new collaborators on the show: Howard Emmett Rogers for the book and J. Keirn Brennan, with whom Friml also worked in Hollywood, for the lyrics. The familiar face in all this was Arthur Hammerstein's, the show's producer.

Based on Richard Walton Tully's 1912 play *The Bird of Paradise*, the story concerns an interracial romance. Luana, a South Sea island princess, marries an American, Paul Wilson, and when he deserts her, she commits suicide by jumping into a volcano. She, as a Pacific islander, is made to pay for loving a white man. As in *Rose Marie* and *The White Eagle*, the interracial liaison results in tragedy. Looking ahead, the show's Pacific setting and race-related theme anticipate those of Rodgers and Hammerstein's *South Pacific*.

Friml's music for *Luana* contained a handful of impressive songs, including "A Son of a Sun," "Yankyula," and "My Bird of Paradise," but the overall score was not one of the composer's most inspired creations. As the unnamed reviewer for the *New York Times* asserted, "The South Sea locale has not stimulated Mr. Friml's natural talent for melody and romantic composing."[11]

Luana closed on October 4 after only twenty-one performances, and Hammerstein blamed the New York Theatre League and the lack of advance-sale tickets for its quick demise. In a desperate effort to keep the show open, Hammerstein reduced the price of orchestra tickets from $6.60 to $5.50.[12] But even with such drastic measures, he was still forced to close the show.

Music Hath Charms (December 29, 1934, Majestic Theatre), Friml's last Broadway operetta, did not fare much better, for it lasted only twenty-nine performances. This was a decidedly old-fashioned operetta mounted by the Shuberts, the leading operetta producers of the second and third decades of the century. The book and lyrics by Rowland Leigh, George Rosener, and John Shubert concerned Maria, Marchese Del Monte Nee Di Orsano, who decides to marry her American suitor, Charles Parker, after hearing the story of her great-grandparents, the Duke of Orsano and the fishermaid Maria Sovrani, also known as "Annina."[13] Set in Venice, the operetta moves from 1934 to 1770 and back again, with the same actors playing the romantic leads in both centuries.

Two years before the appearance of *Music Hath Charms*, the Shuberts purchased the rights to all of the works produced by Arthur Hammerstein for seven hundred dollars, a package that included *The Firefly* and *Rose Marie*.[14] The Shuberts and Friml were thus familiar with each other before they worked together on *Music Hath Charms*.

During its pre-Broadway tryout, when the show was called *Annina*, opera star Maria Jeritza and emerging singing sensation Allan Jones led the cast.[15] (Allan Jones introduced "The Donkey Serenade," with Friml's music, three years later in the 1937 film *The Firefly*.) The original leads were replaced by experienced Broadway singers Natalie Hall and Robert Halliday, the latter having already created the roles of the Red Shadow/Pierre in *The Desert Song* and Robert Misson in *The New Moon*, both with scores by Sigmund Romberg.

Music Hath Charms has numerous links to Romberg. Not only did it tell its story in a way that bore a resemblance to *Maytime*, but it also had one of Romberg's most famous leading men as its star. If this were not enough, the Shuberts, the producers with whom Romberg worked most frequently and most closely, mounted the show. Everything about the show seemed to point to the existence of a Romberg score, not a Friml one.

Critics panned the operetta, including Friml's score. Gilbert W. Gabriel wrote in the *New York American* that the music "is expertly reminiscent of pretty nearly any and every other collection of romantic operetta music," while Atkinson, in the *New York Times*, called Friml's score, as well as just about everything in the show, "routine."[16] The score's highlight was the emotive duet "Exquisite Moment," sung by the romantic leads in their eighteenth-century incarnations from adjacent balconies.

Of Friml's Broadway shows after *The Vagabond King*, only *The Three Musketeers* was a success. Musical theater was changing, as was evident in the work of George Gershwin, whose triumphs included *Girl Crazy* (1930)—which introduced Ethel Merman belting "I Got Rhythm"—and the Pulitzer Prize–winning *Of Thee I Sing* (1930), and Cole Porter, whose *Anything Goes* (1934) was filled with brassy character types far from those in a Friml operetta. Friml could not see the appeal of a show that did not include a crowd-pleasing hero like François Villon or d'Artagnan or nearly operatic music. He refused to adapt to the unashamedly modern Broadway musical comedy paradigm that began to dominate Broadway in the 1930s. But although Friml's star had faded on Broadway, it was rising in California, where the composer permanently relocated in 1934.

6 | Away from Broadway

FRIML'S BROADWAY successes provided him with fame and financial security. But there is much more to Friml than a composer for the musical stage, as is already evident from his early career. From the 1920s on, his activities continued to extend well beyond the walls of a Broadway theater and included writing film and concert music, resuming his career as a performing pianist, and finding personal happiness in his marriage to Kay Ling. These various dimensions of Rudolf Friml complement one another, just as the multiple musical styles in his classic operettas work together to create a well-woven fabric.

Film Musicals

Friml wrote complete scores for two original film musicals, *The Lottery Bride* (1930, Art Cinema Corporation) and *Northwest Outpost* (1947, Republic Pictures), the former starring Jeanette MacDonald and the latter Nelson Eddy. Although Friml never wrote expressly for "America's Singing Sweethearts," the legendary Hollywood duo appeared together in the 1936 film version of *Rose-Marie*. In 1937, between the two original film musicals, came the film version of Friml's first Broadway hit, *The Firefly*, but with a completely new story and a great deal of new music. The film, which starred MacDonald and Allan Jones (who also appeared in *Rose-Marie*), differs enough from the original that it needs to be considered as a separate entity. Friml's Hollywood musicals reflect the same fundamental plan as his Broadway shows: songs define character and relate to the plot, and, when appropriate, specific geographic atmospheres are created through readily identifiable musical tropes.

THE LOTTERY BRIDE

Friml's first film musical, as well as one of the earliest original works in the genre, was *The Lottery Bride*. Broadway veteran and frequent Friml collaborator Arthur Hammerstein produced the film, billed as "An Arthur Hammerstein Operetta" on the opening title, in the hopes of transferring his successful stage reputation to the silver screen. Herbert Stothart created the screenplay, basing it on his original story *Bride 66*, and J. Keirn Brennan was lyricist. The noteworthy Karl Freund was the cinematographer. Freund, born in Bohemia (like Friml), filmed F. W. Murnua's *Der letzte Mann* (The Last Man, 1924) and Fritz Lang's *Metropolis* (1927) in Germany before going to Hollywood, where he helped perfect Technicolor's color processing and later developed television's three-camera system. The much-publicized final scene, shot in newly emerging Technicolor, thanks to Freund, took place underneath a blazing aurora borealis. The film was Jeanette MacDonald's first headliner role but her second appearance in a Friml film, for earlier that same year she played opposite Dennis King in the film version of *The Vagabond King* (see chapter 4).

Unfortunately, *The Lottery Bride* was a commercial and artistic failure. Soon after its release, Hammerstein returned to Broadway, more than a bit embarrassed because this, his only effort in the film industry, turned out to be one of his greatest artistic disappointments. MacDonald later recalled that the film's only redeeming quality was the fun she had on the set with costars Joe E. Brown and ZaSu Pitts.[1]

In Stothart's story, Jenny Trondson (MacDonald), a singer at the Viking Ship, a student haunt in Oslo, is in love with Chris Svenson (John Garrick). Her friend Hilda (Pitts) runs the club and has recently hired American Hoke Curtis (Brown) and his band to play for a dance marathon. Jenny's younger brother Nels (Carroll Nye) tells her that he embezzled money in order to support his gambling habit and begs her to enter the dance marathon with him since he needs the money they would win in order to repay Alberto. Alberto, after seeing Jenny, tells Nels that he will erase the debt if Jenny will grant him sexual favors. Nels and Jenny refuse Alberto's offer and enter the marathon. During a break, Nels escapes through a window and Jenny, heartbroken, rests her head on Alberto's chest. Chris enters, misinterprets what he sees, and leaves in a fury. The police suspect Jenny in Nels's escape and arrest her. After Hilda and Hoke pay her bail, she becomes a picture bride and heads north to a mining camp, along with Hilda and Hoke.

In the recreation hall of the King's Bay Mining Company, the miners are holding a lottery for brides. Chris tells his brother Olaf (Robert Chisolm), the foreman, that he wants nothing to do with marriage, since he came north to forget a woman in Oslo. But Olaf persuades Chris to enter the lottery anyway, and Chris draws Bride 66 (hence the title of the original story). Of course, Bride 66 is Jenny. Chris gives the card with her picture to Olaf without looking at it. As Jenny arrives at the camp, she recognizes Chris and smiles at him; he returns her greeting with an icy glare. Olaf introduces his picture bride to his brother, and the former lovers pretend that it is their first meeting.

A dirigible on its way to the North Pole, piloted by none other than Alberto, lands at the mining camp. Chris decides to join Alberto on the dirigible, leaving Olaf, who, Chris realizes, deeply loves Jenny, to be with her. Soon after the dirigible takes off, Olaf discovers a photo of Chris and Jenny together and realizes their history and the sacrifice Chris has made. Moments later, the dirigible crashes but does not explode. Undaunted by the winter storms, Olaf ventures into the ice to find his brother. Meanwhile, Jenny convinces the miners to take an icebreaker and search for survivors. Olaf finds his brother and Alberto just before the icebreaker arrives, with Jenny on the prow. Jenny and Chris gaze longingly at each other as their love is reignited under the aurora borealis.

Central to the score are its two love waltzes, "You're an Angel" and "My Northern Light," both of which are heard during the opening credits. One waltz belongs to each brother as an expression of his love for Jenny: the former to Olaf and the latter to Chris. "My Northern Light" recurs throughout the film; this only makes sense since it is Chris who will be with Jenny at the end of the story. After its initial appearance early in the film, it returns near the end of the dance marathon in a primitivist styling with jazz influences. The waltz also appears as instrumental underscoring for the scene in which Olaf finds the picture of Jenny and Chris and again in the final sequence as the lovers spy each other.

As an operetta film, *The Lottery Bride* needed a male choral march. But since the story did not include an appropriate dramatic function for such a number, it was necessary to find another way to fit a heroic-themed march into the scenario. Friml ended up writing a duet for Olaf and Chris, eventually supported by the male chorus. The song, "Shoulder to Shoulder," glorifies brotherly camaraderie and support. Brothers will remain loyal "through hell and high water" and will fight together "shoulder to shoulder." The title is identical to one of the alternative titles for Sigmund Romberg's "Stouthearted Men" from *The New Moon* and in fact turns into that type of song during the final refrain when the male chorus enters. The difference here, though, is that the spirit of the song lacks any relevance to social issues and overcoming injustice.

The opening sequence at the Viking Ship resembles the opening numbers at Lady Jane's Hotel in *Rose Marie* and the Fir Cone Tavern in *The Vagabond King*. Revelry is the key ingredient here; student carousing is engagingly set to music and dance. The film begins with "Come Drink to the Girl That You Love," a short, energetic choral number complete with pounding mugs, student hats, and a grandiose toast at its conclusion. Modeled on the "Drinking Song" from *The Student Prince*, Romberg's Teutonic operetta from 1924, Friml's incarnation does not limit the revelers to men but rather includes a chorus of both men and women (as do the opening choruses of *Rose Marie* and *The Vagabond King*). Jenny enters, leading the female chorus in "Yubla," a lighthearted dance routine that establishes the Viking Ship as a venue where young men come to be entertained.

The dance marathon sequence showcases the possibilities of dance on-screen and is an important precedent for choreographic film musicals such as *42nd Street* (1933) and *Gold Diggers of 1933* (1933). It also endorsed the popularity of dance marathons in 1930, when *The Lottery Bride* was released. These tests of physical endurance were extremely well known during the 1920s and 1930s, and many watching the film would have eagerly participated in them.

The film had little, if anything, to do with Nordic culture, aside from the name of the inn (Viking Ship) and the fact that mining did take place in the northern part of Norway. The reason for placing the story in the extreme north had to do with the inherent possibilities of film technology: the film had to be set near the Arctic Circle in order to include the aurora borealis in the final scene, and the aurora borealis in turn was an excuse to showcase the marvels of Technicolor.

Among the finest vocal performances in the film are those by Australian-English baritone Robert Chisholm, who played Olaf. This was Chisholm's only American film appearance.[2] His music included the waltz "You're an Angel" and the ballad "I'll Follow the Trail," an anthem of self-determination to persevere amid great difficulty and turmoil. Chisholm had an especially resonant upper register, something that comes through in the film. His voice recorded well, and his performance in *The Lottery Bride* is one of the vocal highlights of early musical cinema.

THE FIREFLY

When MGM filmed *The Firefly* in 1937, all that remained of the original operetta was a handful of songs. The story was completely recast as a protest again dictatorial oppression in Spain. The screenwriters, Ogden Nash, Frances Goodrich, and Albert Hackett, were all sympathetic to the Republican efforts against Fascism in the Spanish Civil War, which had erupted in July of the previous year, and wanted the new film to show their political leanings.[3]

The revised storyline, set in 1808 and based on A. L. F. Schaumann's memoirs *On the Road with Wellington* (published in English in 1924), focused on Nina Maria (Jeanette MacDonald), "The Firefly," a Spanish spy who lures Napoleon's officers through song and dance and ultimately assists in the defeat of the French at Vittoria. Along the way, she falls in love with Don Diego Manrique de Lara (Allan Jones), who is in reality a French spy. After Don Diego betrays Nina when she is caught carrying a strategic map, she confesses to him that the map is a fake and that she was supposed to get caught in order to feed misinformation to Napoleon's army. But it is too late, for thanks to the French moving their armies according to what they found on Nina's map, the combined Spanish and English forces drive Napoleon out of Spain. After the battle of Vittoria, Nina finds Don Diego in a field hospital, and since the war is over, the lovers can be together.

Studio dictates determined the film's production and overall aesthetic. In 1937, MGM, under the leadership of Leonard B. Mayer, decided that the Jeanette MacDonald musicals would be not only entertainment but also vehicles meant to advance the cultural life of filmgoers and would likewise strengthen the studio's self-image of respectability.[4] This aesthetic goal prompted many decisions regarding *The Firefly*. In MacDonald's "He Who Loves and Runs Away," for example, costume designer Adrian dressed the star in an androgynous costume inspired by the images of Aubrey Beardsley and the overall Art Nouveau style.[5] The nightmarish shots depicting French brutality were modeled after the work of Francisco de Goya, and the scenic landscape images followed the style of the seventeenth-century religious painter Bartolomé Murillo.[6]

Only four songs from the stage production made it into the film: "Love Is Like a Firefly," "When a Maid Comes Knocking at Your Heart," "Sympathy," and "Giannina Mia." These songs could all be easily extracted from a show about a cross-dressed street singer on her way to Bermuda and put into one about Napoleonic wars in Spain; they were not tied as closely to the plot as songs from Friml's later shows would be. Of particular interest is "Giannina Mia": in the stage ver-

Allan Jones and Jeanette MacDonald on the set of The Firefly. *Hulton Archive, John Kobal Foundation / Getty Images.*

sion it was a coloratura vehicle for Emma Trentini, but in the film, Allan Jones sings it to showcase his tenor voice. Since the film is better known than the stage play, more people are likely to associate the song with a male voice. "Sympathy" remains a duet, but this time the leads, MacDonald and Jones, sing it, as opposed to the secondary couple in the stage version.

Friml and Harbach wrote three new songs for the film: "He Who Loves and Runs Away," a habanera that morphs into a march, and two songs led by Jones after MacDonald dazzles an on-screen audience with "Love Is Like a Firefly," the bolero "When the Wine is Full of Fire," and the waltz "A Woman's Kiss." The habanera and bolero endorse the film's Spanish setting, affirming its difference from the stage version.

But the most memorable and important new song for the film was "The Donkey Serenade." In the film, Jones, on horseback, sings the song to MacDonald as she is riding in a carriage. The song became a foxtrot, thanks to MGM music director Herbert Stothart's arrangement, and numerous Hispanic instruments were added to the orchestration in order to suggest a sense of place, including Cuban "bimbos" (a form of marimba with wooden tubes and attachments to give a buzzing noise), two zithers, six Mexican guitars, Cuban maracas, and gourd tom-toms.[7] None of these was truly Spanish, but together they were effective in their Hispanic exoticism.

Pedro, the coachman who accompanies the song, is not just any coachman but rather Manuel Alvarez Maciste, the Mexican guitarist-tenor who had previously appeared in MGM's *The Gay Desperado* (1936) and who was especially known for his flamenco playing.[8] The coachman's son Juan (Robert Sindola) also participates in the song by playing a short refrain on an albodoniga, a Mexican clay fife that Stothart bought in Mexico especially for the film. The fife tune became, along with Jones's singing, a quintessential feature of the song.[9]

The manner in which the song made it into the film was fraught with difficulties. Friml unexpectedly entered the sound studio on the day that Jones was recording "The Donkey Serenade" after learning that Chet Forrest and Bob Wright had written lyrics to his solo piano piece "Chanson" and that Stothart, in his musical arrangement, had increased its tempo. The gentle love song was now a comic lovesick lament. Friml stormed onto the recording stage and bellowed, "Zot is not Friml!" The next day, he brought a five million dollar copyright infringement suit against MGM that was settled out of court.[10]

MGM reused "The Donkey Serenade" in the patriotic feature *Anchors Aweigh* (1945), this time as an instrumental feature. Although the film starred Frank Sinatra, Gene Kelly, and Kathryn Grayson, it was not any of these stars who intoned the song. Rather, José Iturbi and his orchestra are seen recording it on a MGM soundstage. In this arrangement for solo piano and orchestra, Iturbi is the soloist. Axel Stordahl's orchestration includes a prominent oboe solo, recalling the heckelphone of Ferde Grofé's "Chansonette" arrangement. The song appears in a diegetic "concert" context and is thus separated from the film's overall dramatic narrative. It is featured as a piece of 1940s popular music to be enjoyed in and of itself.

The film version of *The Firefly* returned to the live stage in Prague in 1973 as *Španělská vyzvědačka* (The Spanish Spy), which opened at the Karlín Theatre on April 26. This was five months after Friml died, so he never saw the production. His widow attended the opening night performance, however, and delivered kind words about how much she knew her husband would have enjoyed it.

Friml's first original film musical starred Jeanette MacDonald, and so it somehow seems fitting that his only other original work in the genre featured Nelson Eddy. *Northwest Outpost* paired Eddy with the Hungarian mezzo-soprano Ilona Massey; the two singing stars had previously appeared together in *Rosalie* (1937) and *Balalaika* (1939).[11] Like *Balalaika*, *Northwest Outpost* features Russians as the principal dramatic characters and has a plot about good defeating evil.

Set during the nineteenth century at Fort Ross, the main Russian trading post in California at the time, the film begins with a chorus of male convicts singing the plaintive "Weary." The aristocratic Natalie (Massey) arrives from Russia, although no one, including Nikolai, the post's commander, is sure why she is there. American captain James Laurence (Eddy) enters, leading the male chorus, all of whom are on horseback, in the heroic march "One More Mile to Go." Natalie hears James's beautiful voice, and the two fall in love almost immediately. A convict ship arrives, and among the prisoners is Igor Savin, a Russian criminal whom Natalie was blackmailed into marrying. Natalie, it is learned, came to Fort Ross looking for him. Savin bargains with the head guard, Volkoff, for his escape, and Natalie, wanting to rid herself of Savin and his influence, gives him her jewels. Igor and Volkoff escape to a Chinese ship, and after Natalie's tangential involvement with the men is discovered, she is banished from Fort Ross and also makes her way to the departing boat. James tracks the criminals and, with Nikolai's help, kills them. The film ends with Natalie and James riding off together on horseback, leading the chorus, also paired off and riding horses, happily singing "Love Is the Time," a buoyant waltz that Natalie introduced earlier in the film.

The story has many similarities to *Rose Marie*, especially the 1936 film version: an officer of the law falls in love with a woman who is associated with a suspected criminal. Furthermore, both have Western settings and scores that include specific ethnic identifiers, Indian in *Rose Marie* and Russian and Chinese in *Northwest Outpost*.

Friml evokes particular ethnicities in three instances in the film, two of which are Russian and one of which is Chinese. A balalaika orchestra accompanies Natalie on-screen in her ballad "Raindrops on a Drum," providing aural and visual monikers for her character's ethnicity. Later, a Russian Easter vigil is enacted during which James sings to organ accompaniment. This sequence, meant to be evocative, is woefully inauthentic, for a traditional Orthodox service would be sung by a choir, not a soloist, and certainly would not include an organ. The third example, the Chinese one, takes place aboard the Chinese ship, where Friml creates a remarkably accurate Oriental sound world through pitch-bending and a combination of bowed and plucked Asian instruments.

The film is unashamed Cold War Hollywood propaganda about American superiority and Soviet (as Russian) inferiority. The pro-American view is immediately evident during the opening credits, when "The American G.I. Chorus" sings the ballad "Raindrops on a Drum." According to a title card, "This group was organized by Major Herbert Wall and is composed entirely of Ex-G.I.'s who served on every battlefront of the world during World War II. These men are the proud bearers of 452 decorations awarded by the various branches of the Armed Forces in which they served."

The chorus appears throughout the film. After all, what would an operetta be, onstage or on-screen, without a male chorus? And who better to lead them than the all-American Nelson Eddy? His military uniform and persona were by this time tropes for the screen actor. He was a Canadian Mountie in *Rose-Marie*, a West Point cadet in *Rosalie*, and a U.S. Army lieutenant in *The Girl of the Golden West*. He was a true American patriotic freedom-fighter in *Let Freedom Ring* (1939), where he led the rousing Romberg march "Where Else but Here?"

Friml's heroic march in *Northwest Outpost* is "One More Mile to Go." The male choral number follows the tradition of "The Mounties" in *Rose Marie* and "Song of the Vagabonds" in *The Vagabond King*, not only in general spirit but also through its sections in the minor mode. The lyrics are different from those of its predecessors, however. Here, the song appears during a homecoming; men who have fought tyranny and injustice are returning home to the women they love and are counting down the miles to their arrival. The lyric would have certainly resonated with the military veterans in the audience, including those singing in the film's chorus.

The song's placement in the film is also part of a Nelson Eddy trope, where the actor's initial appearance is as leader of a male chorus who fights oppression. His entrance on horseback is nearly identical to that in *The Girl of Golden West*, which is also set in nineteenth-century California but has a score by Romberg rather than Friml and costars MacDonald rather than Massey.

Natalie, as a Russian aristocrat, sings some hauntingly beautiful music, including the unhurried ballads "Tell Me with Your Eyes" and "Raindrops on a Drum" and the vivacious waltz "Love Is the Time." Considering that Massey sang at the Vienna Staatsoper and had a stunning voice, Friml certainly must have enjoyed writing for her.

Aside from Natalie, the Russians in the film are portrayed as oppressors who treat political prisoners brutally and who operate according to principles of blackmail and corruption; these nineteenth-century Russians are foils for their twentieth-century Soviet successors. The film's first musical number is "Weary," a lament sung by the prisoners at Fort Ross. The minor mode recurs throughout the film whenever treachery and injustice are present; it can easily be interpreted as representing the plight of the Soviet people.

Friml was extremely concerned about the spread of Communism, for his native land had fallen under Communist rule. He was constantly appreciative of the freedom he enjoyed in America. *Northwest Outpost*, therefore, concerned an issue that held great personal significance for Friml: the defeat of political corruption and oppression.

Living Life

Friml lived life to its fullest. He credited his ninety-plus years to regular physical exercise. His Hollywood residence was at the top of Lookout Mountain, and one of his favorite routines was to bicycle fifteen miles to Santa Monica for a swim, then bicycle back.[12] This becomes all the more impressive when one realizes that the return journey was uphill. He also stood on his head twice daily for ten minutes, had his wife walk on his back as a form of massage, and took brisk walks.[13] Furthermore, it was his practice to avoid heavy meals in the evening and to get plenty of rest.[14]

On April 17, 1952, Friml married his true love, Kay Wong Ling, his Chinese American secretary of fourteen years. He was seventy-two; she was thirty-nine. As Mrs. Friml wrote: "My life with Rudolf was a happy one and I was fortunate in being able to share so many lovely years with him."[15] It was her first marriage and his fourth. The three previous Mrs. Frimls had all divorced him.

Friml's first marriage, to Mathilde "Tillie" Baruch, took place in Los Angeles on May 26, 1909. The couple had two children, Rudolf Jr., who later went on to work in the music departments at both Warner Brothers and Universal Studios, and Marie Lucille. Friml dedicated his *California Suite* for piano, op. 57 (1910), to Mathilde. The acrimonious divorce in 1915 was covered in the papers, for part of the suit involved Mathilde suing Emma Trentini, star of *The Firefly* and *The Peasant Girl*, for stealing her husband's affections. Trentini responded, in no uncertain terms, that this could not be, for all the affection Rudolf had for Mathilde had long since vanished when she and Rudolf met and, as she admitted, had a relationship.[16]

The second Mrs. Friml was Blanch Betters, an actress who had been in the chorus of *Katinka*. Their marriage lasted two years, and its end had an unforeseen consequence: the denial of Friml's application to become a U.S. citizen. On July 14, 1921, the New York County Supreme Court's judge refused the composer's petition on the grounds that his second wife had divorced him.[17] (Friml did succeed in becoming a U.S. citizen in 1925.)

Friml's third wife was actress Elsie Lawson. She played the maid in Friml's *Glorianna*, and Friml dedicated his *Love Messages: Five Pieces for Piano*, published in 1919, to her. Elsie wrote lyrics for Friml's song "Longing" (1923) and was the mother of his third and youngest child, William.[18]

After three failed marriages, finding happiness with Kay certainly meant a great deal to the successful Broadway composer. As he told her, "I don't remember any of my other three wives, you are the only one who is really my wife."[19] Their marriage lasted until his death in 1972.

The Frimls loved to travel. They spent the last two months of 1956 in Hawaii,

Rudolf and Kay Friml posing aboard the ocean liner Cristoforo Colombo, *1954. Copyright Bettman / Corbis.*

where Rudolf played concerts and entertained patients at the army hospital in Honolulu.[20] According to the *Hollywood Reporter,* he also completed his autobiography in Hawaii and sent it to Henry Holt and Company.[21] The volume was never published, although Friml's typescript recollections survive.[22]

The couple also enjoyed living in California and maintained three homes in the state: one in Hollywood, one in San Francisco, and one in Desert Palms, near Palm Springs. The Hollywood home, at the top of Lookout Mountain, was a former residence of Ginger Rogers. The large Spanish-style hacienda offered spectacular views from its large living room, where Friml often hired Hollywood studio musicians to come and record his latest creations. The San Francisco residence was in picturesque Sutro Heights, and the Desert Palms home was, according to Friml, their "retreat from the smog."

Friml relished his celebrity status. He played for American presidents Theodore Roosevelt, Calvin Coolidge, Harry S. Truman, John F. Kennedy, and Lyndon B. Johnson and was invited to play at the White House on three separate occasions.[23] He especially enjoyed his time with Truman, whose musical tastes were similar to his own. Truman told Friml that he didn't like "noisy" music, which Friml took to mean jazz. He preferred classical composers, especially Chopin, who was also one of Friml's idols. When Truman told Friml that he played Chopin's C-sharp minor waltz, Friml amicably retorted, "I thought you played the Missouri Waltz only."[24]

The Pianist and Improviser

Friml was at the piano for four to six hours a day, even in his nineties. He would awaken early and play a couple of hours before breakfast. In 1950, Friml published the three-volume *How I Keep My Technique,* a series of advanced technical studies for solo piano.[25] Exercises for all aspects of piano playing—scales, arpeggios, articulations, velocity, and much more—appear in the volumes. Each piece is a freestanding work that requires considerable technical skill. At the beginning of each study is a short descriptor of its purpose. These include remarks such as: "Study for melody in left hand with arpeggios in right hand" (vol. 1, part 1, no. 7), "Melody in both hands predominates while accompaniment is subdued" (vol. 1, part 1, no. 13; vol. 1, part 2, no. 3), "To develop precision in chord playing" (vol. 1, part 2, no. 6), and "An etude for facility in staccato and arpeggio playing" (vol. 2, no. 14). In every case, a melody, Friml's trademark, is at its center.

From the time of his early concerts in the first decade of the twentieth century, improvisations were a mainstay of Friml's musical productivity. He would frequently wake up in the middle of the night with a tune in his head. Unable to sleep, he would have to go downstairs to the piano to develop the tune. He would often record himself so that he could remember what he had done. He (or others) transcribed a number of these improvisations, giving them inventive titles such as "A G.I. in St. Peter's Cathedral in Rome," "Starlight Improvisation," "Souvenir de Hollywood," "Cannonball Dance," "Samba Boogie," and the especially intriguingly titled "Satanic Musings, Valse de Concert." Hundreds of reel-to-reel tapes of improvisations filled the closets in the Frimls' Hollywood home.[26]

Friml constantly had music going through his head, pounding to get out. People often remarked to him how wonderful it must be to always hear music playing, especially his music. Friml responded that it wasn't wonderful at all; in fact, he often wished he could turn it off because it drove him crazy.[27] Once, he even went so far as to call it a disease.[28]

He continued to perform publicly well into his eighties, and his performances attracted legions of loyal fans. Milton Berliner, in the *Washington Daily News*, wrote about a concert Friml gave at the Carter Barron Amphitheater on June 28, 1965: "Mr. Friml, who came on early to do 20 minutes at the piano before the company of singers and dancers did scenes from his famous operettas, stayed on for close to 40. . . . No wonder. The 85–year-old composer did a cascade of runs and trills and variations on 'Indian Love Call' and other hits of his that would have done credit to a far younger man. You really have to hear it to believe it."[29] During the concert, Friml played not only his own music but also Chopin's Fantasie-Impromptu and a selection of Czech folk songs, the latter to the great delight of the Czech Americans in the audience.[30]

In 1966, just two months before his eighty-seventh birthday, Friml delighted audiences in Coral Gables, Florida. He was supposed to play a forty-five-minute program at the Musicians Club of America, but because so many people turned up for the concert, Friml ended up playing his program twice in back-to-back performances. Reviewing the recital, Doris Reno wrote in the *Miami Herald*: "Friml is an amazingly virile executant at the keyboard, though he is not competing with any of today's virtuosos. His fingers are agile, and he can play both loud and fast."[31] The virtuosity and commanding stage presence of Friml's youth were still intact.

Friml's interpretations of the music of other composers were very much his own. As Kay Friml said, "He played Chopin his way."[32] Concert reviewers agreed. Hyphenated descriptors for the composer of a work were completely appropriate, as in the following commentary from a concert in 1966: "When performing the classics, he works in his own little roulades whenever he finds a vacancy in the original score, and his main object seems to be to keep things alive and moving dramatically forward. . . . When he plays the classics, he turns out Chopin-Friml or Smetana-Friml with the greatest possible dash and verve."[33]

Another reviewer commented, on a different occasion: "The two best offerings of the evening were Friml's rendition of Chopin's 'Valse Celebre,' which he more or less played as written, and the 'Going Home' theme from Antonín Dvořák's 'New World Symphony.'"[34] The reviewer seemed surprised that the Chopin sounded like Chopin. Friml's gifts at improvisation and elaboration were obviously not limited to the privacy of his home tape recorder. In his public performances, he continued and endorsed the late-nineteenth-century Romantic tradition of a virtuoso musician by infusing his performances with an unmistakable personal flair.

Friml owned two Steinway pianos that sat near each other in his living room. One went to the Czech Museum of Music, a unit of the National Museum in Prague; the other resides at the Nixon Presidential Library in Yorba Linda, California, where it is used for concerts. Nixon was president when Friml died in 1972, and a memorial plaque to Friml also hangs at the library.

Songs

Friml wrote a number of independent songs, ones not specifically intended for a stage or screen production. "L'amour, toujours, l'amour" (Love Everlasting), with its languid 6/4 refrain and evocative lyrics by Catherine Chisholm Cushing (Friml's librettist for *Glorianna*), became one of Friml's most frequently performed works. Written in 1922, its legacy parallels that of "Chansonette," for it too was a favorite with various types of instrumental ensembles, including small orchestras. The song appeared in several Hollywood films, increasing its popularity. One example of this treatment is in *This Is the Life* (1944, Universal), in which Susanna Foster sings it in her role of Angela, an eighteen-year-old ingenue who is in love with the fortyish Patric Knowles (Hilary Jarret). The title was also appropriated for Dailey Paskman's proposed film treatment of Friml's life and William Osteck's idea for a stage revue featuring Friml's songs and reminiscences about the composer.[35]

Decades later, Friml dedicated the solo piano piece "So You Are—Trés charmant" and subsequent song "Jacqueline" to Jacqueline Kennedy in 1963 on the occasion of her thirty-fourth birthday. The song uses the same melody as the piano piece, and Forman Brown crafted a bilingual (French and English) lyric for the graceful waltz melody that extols the merits of the cultured First Lady. Jacqueline Kennedy had urbane artistic tastes and was directly involved with planning musical programs at the White House.[36] Friml heard through his agent that Mrs. Kennedy liked the piece but was a bit alarmed when he learned that she had it recorded by the Marine Corps Band, wondering how the gentle, intimate waltz would sound played by a large military wind ensemble.[37]

Large-Scale Works

In the early 1960s, Friml turned his compositional focus toward orchestral works for concert performance.[38] This shift resulted at least in part from what Friml considered to be the deplorable state of the musical theater at the time. All of these orchestral works remain unpublished and have been almost entirely forgotten at the time of this writing. Most are programmatic and have connections to either Czech themes or are musical depictions of various travel destinations.

Friml was very proud of his Czech heritage, and this love for his homeland is at the forefront of several pieces. During his later years, Friml made annual visits to Czechoslovakia (as it was called at the time) to visit his sister, Zdeňka, and afterward would spend time at Karlovy Vary (Karlsbad), a famous Czech spa, to enjoy the baths' physical healing and rejuvenating properties.[39] Kay Friml told of the importance of her husband's homeland when she gave a speech in 1973 in conjunction with the opening of *Španělská vyzvědačka* at Prague's Karlín Theatre: "He truly loved his country and its courageous people with a passionate zeal and devotion. His wealth of training and musicianship he ascribed to his good fortune and having Antonín Dvořák as his mentor and teacher. In all his concerts and creative efforts he proudly referred to the inspiration of Dvořák."[40] She told another audience on the same visit: "He was proud of his Czech heritage. He had not forgotten the language and always [spoke] Czech with his countrymen in America."[41]

Among Friml's Czech-inspired works is *Scenes from My Youth* (1962), a programmatic depiction of a day in Prague. It opens at sunrise as three solo woodwinds—the clarinet onstage, the flute backstage left, and the oboe backstage right—exchange early morning greetings. Subsequent sections depict the hustle and bustle of the streets and market, respite in the parks and gardens, romantic infatuation, church bells, a wind band, a winter scene (complete with sleigh bells in the orchestra), various sorts of dances, a majestic sunset—perhaps over Vyšerad, the legendary burial place of Czech heroes, which is also the final image in Smetana's *Vltava* (The Moldau)—and a rousing celebratory conclusion. The work, more a suite with sections progressing directly one into another, is cinematic in scope and offers a stunning panoramic vista of fin de siècle Prague.

Slavonic Rhapsody, first performed by Arthur Fiedler and the San Francisco Symphony on August 14, 1962, consists of vignettes based on Czech folk music and, like *Scenes from My Youth*, is dedicated to Dvořák. The reviewer for the *San Francisco Examiner* was very impressed with the modestly proportioned work, writing "at times it is splendidly guttural, at times as breathtaking as Dvořák ever was. It is one of those small-scale works that endure through their very simplicity and pure, unaffected emotionalism, and it would not surprise me if it is heard often in the future."[42]

Other Czech-themed works include *Czech Rhapsody*, op. 125, a large-scale work in the late Romantic nationalist style;[43] *Little Czech Concerto*, a sprightly one-movement work for piano and orchestra; and the *Bohemian Club Concerto* for piano and orchestra, a three-movement concerto in the Romantic vein dedicated to the San Francisco Bohemian Club.[44] The list also includes *Slavonic Memories*,[45] *Moravian Festival (Festoravia)*,[46] and *Masaryk Rhapsody*, the last in honor of Czecho-slovakia's first president. Broader Habsburg images appear in *Happy Days in Prater* and *Hungarian Kaleidoscope Music*.

Friml loved to travel, as is reflected in several of his later orchestral works. These musical travelogues continue the forays into musical exoticism that made "Allah's Holiday" in *Katinka* and *Rose Marie* so famous.

Exodus to Hong Kong (1961),[47] which had its premiere on the same concert as *Slavonic Rhapsody* with Fiedler and the San Francisco Symphony in 1962, is a fast-paced journey that drives toward a musical depiction of the famous port. Images shift quickly, causing one reviewer to remark that the piece was like experiencing "flashing glimpses of the Hong Kong countryside through the windows of a speeding train."[48] The combination of European-based harmonies with Oriental-evoking percussion and brass orchestration gave a blended cultural portrayal of the then-British (and culturally blended) colony.

Friml wrote his descriptive symphonic poem *Matterhorn* (1962)[49] after seeing the imposing mountain. The experience inspired a theme, which Friml immediately wrote down. He completed the work in Lucerne, where he was staying at the time.[50] The piece captures the commanding presence, ruggedness, splendor, and poise of its subject. Friml dedicated the work to the memory of John F. Kennedy after the president's assassination, for he saw great strength in both the man and the mountain.

In 1968, Rudolf and Kay Friml had an audience with Pope Paul VI. While

*Friml in St. Mark's
Square, Venice.
Courtesy of
Kay Friml.*

in Rome, Rudolf conducted two Rome-inspired works: *The Bells of Rome*[51] and *Prelude to Vatican City. The Bells of Rome* includes ten mandolins in its orchestration. Friml certainly wanted to create local color! Near the end of the work is a virtuoso exposed piano part during which Friml could showcase his exceptional pianistic abilities.

Other Czech-themed works from the 1960s include *San Francisco Bay— Fantasy for Orchestra*,[52] a short atmospheric work in an Impressionist style. It includes characteristically French orchestral effects such as tremolo strings along with muted strings and trumpets. Also in this vein are *Serenata a un toro* (Serenade to a Bull),[53] where the solo bassoon is the bull, *Bouquet Brazil*,[54] and *Aborigines' Holiday.*[55]

Friml also composed a handful of choral works. In the sacred music realm, the ten-minute Easter cantata *The Stone Is Rolled Away* (1943) is a celebratory retelling of the resurrection of Christ scored for the large forces of six soloists, choir, and orchestra, with optional organ.[56] In 1950, Friml created a choral arrangement of the African American spiritual "Don't Take My Jesus Away," following his teacher Dvořák's exhortation to his students on the merits of African American music. In a contrasting vein is the fifteen-minute *Spirit of America* (1963), a patriotic celebration for large orchestra and chorus that concludes with a spectacular display of orchestral fireworks. Friml envisioned this as a tribute to his own immigrant experience.[57]

Through these works for concert performance, especially those for orchestra, Friml made an aesthetic return to the days of his youth. His compositional style in these pieces, as in his early works, was firmly rooted in a late-nineteenth-century Romantic style akin to that of his teacher, Dvořák. He was perfectly content to ignore the musical developments of the twentieth century. Just as he remained dedicated to the vaulting musical styles of the second and third decades in his musical theater works, even when they became "outdated," so did he continue his allegiance to the glorious world of turn-of-the-century Prague in his concert music, despite—or, considering Friml's stubbornness, in spite of—substantial shifts in musical style. He knew what he enjoyed and always remained true to himself.

Rudolf Friml passed away on Sunday, November 12, 1972, at 11:05 P.M. Kay Friml called that day "the saddest day of my life."[58] Friml's funeral took place at Blessed Sacrament Catholic Church in Hollywood on November 16. He was buried at Forest Lawn Memorial Park in Glendale.

7 | Reputation and Legacy

ALTHOUGH RUDOLF FRIML had a successful multifaceted musical career, he is best remembered for his Broadway operettas from the second and third decades of the twentieth century. But even the reputations of these works have faded from their previous glory. Why is this the case? Friml recalled Russell Janney, with whom he collaborated on *June Love*, *The Vagabond King*, and *The White Eagle*, telling him the answer: "It's the damn operetta librettos that die. That was Victor Herbert's tragedy. Great music, great songs in stupid stories. It's up to me to find you *a story* that won't die—that will stand up to the kind of music I know you can give it."[1]

Inherently problematic and often dated librettos pose great challenges for those who want to revive Broadway musicals from the first third of the century, including those by Friml. An easy or foolproof solution does not exist. Topical references to popular culture that made the works relevant to their time and kept them popular with contemporary audiences would be lost on most audiences in the early twenty-first century. Humor evolved, acting styles changed, and it became all too easy to interpret operetta with a substantial degree of camp and self-parody that only served to negate the true spirit of the works.

One instance of things going terribly wrong was the 1984 revival of *The Three Musketeers* at the Broadway Theatre. Mark Bramble revised the book, Kirk Nurock adapted the music, and Joe Layton directed the short-lived production of nine performances. Reviews were cruel but made their point: the revival failed. As the reviewer for *Variety* wrote: "The creators obviously found the basic material quaint and spoof-worthy, but have failed to devise an acceptable contemporary approach. A lot of it is cheap and vulgar, and wit there is none."[2] Brendan Gill began his review for the *New Yorker*, appropriately entitled "Grave Robbers," with an especially disparaging image: "'The Three Musketeers,' at the Broadway, is so through-going a disaster that one is constantly tempted to avert one's eyes from it, as from some frightful road-side accident. Out of kindness, a reviewer might be willing to call its miserable heaping up of failed intentions laughable, but the fact of the matter is that the production, lying upon the stage like the colossal wreckage of a Spruce Goose doomed never to fly, yields not even a single rueful smile."[3]

The music was also revised and likewise lost its original power. Erika Munk wrote in a review with the ingenious title "Swashbungled" in the *Village Voice*: "Friml played earnestly would be a hoot; Friml adapted by Kirk Nurock is just a mess."[4] The *Variety* reviewer offered a more positive assessment of the original music but also expressed concern about its handling: "The rousing Friml songs get lusty full-voiced treatment and are the most savory aspect of the show, despite overly brassy orchestrations."[5]

As is so often the case with revivals, the music works—at least most of the time—but the book revisions and performance styles fail. This raises the question as to whether it is worth it even to try to revive these classic operettas. Gill opined that the entire idea of reviving *The Three Musketeers* in 1984 was a bad choice, calling the original a show "that ought to have been allowed to remain out of sight and out of mind, embalmed by time."[6]

While this remark may be more than a bit harsh, Friml's music and aesthetic were certainly firmly and unashamedly rooted in the Broadway styles of the early twentieth century. Even in the 1930s, when new musical styles were emerging, Friml refused to adapt. The new type of musical theater star—the singing actor, as opposed to the acting singer—was not something that pleased the composer. While he wrote successfully for character actors, such as Herman and Lady Jane in *Rose Marie*, these were secondary roles, not the romantic leads.

Friml did not care for what are now considered "Golden Age" musicals such as *Hello, Dolly!* (1964), *Funny Girl* (1964), and *Mame* (1966), dismissing them as "trash."[7] He even walked out on *My Fair Lady* (1956) in London, stating that nobody sang in the show. Neither was he completely enamored with Richard Rodgers, calling him "a clever fellow; he knows how to write a good song—keeps it in one octave. Now I never liked to be limited."[8] Friml wrote his leading roles for operatically trained voices for whom vocal virtuosity was paramount and for whom the musical score was the most important aspect of the performance.

It was not only midcentury musical theater composers whose styles Friml disliked. Regarding Igor Stravinsky, he remarked, "He takes a strain, wraps it in discord and plays it as badly as he can."[9] But he also respected Stravinsky, stating "he had the courage to be different."[10] Of rock and roll, Friml certainly did not hold back his opinion: "It was originated by cannibals."[11] Enough said.

But there were plenty of twentieth-century composers he admired, including Dmitry Shostakovich, Aram Khatchaturian, Heitor Villa-Lobos, and Aaron Copland. Friml appreciated their melody-driven works and remarked, "They are serious composers. Their music will live and be remembered."[12]

In the latter part of the twentieth century, Friml's music became associated with images of nostalgia. His compositions embodied the sounds of earlier, more innocent epochs, and several significant creators of film and fiction have drawn upon these connections in their own work. Director Roman Polanski used Friml's music to create a sense of the passing of time in his film *Chinatown* (1974). "Some Day" and "The Vagabond King Waltz" are heard offscreen as source music in the Mar Vista Rest Home sequence as aural icons of the time when the home's residents were young. The songs emanate from one of the rooms as they are played on an old piano that is out of tune and in desperate need of repair. Their evocative power remains through the hands of the unseen performer.

Woody Allen's film *Radio Days* (1987), constructed as a series of vignettes, consists of stories, all set in the 1940s, that are told in flashback. Nostalgia permeates the film from beginning to end. The sequence about songs begins with "The Donkey Serenade" playing on the radio, over which the narrator recalls how his aunt listened to music and "because of her I grew up hearing the most wonderful songs." Friml's "Donkey Serenade" was at the "head of the class" as far as music was concerned.

Father Andrew M. Greeley included a Friml reference in his 2000 novel *A Christmas Wedding*.[13] The plot centers on newlyweds Chucky O'Malley and Rosemarie, who is also the groom's foster sister. While children, they would sing "Rose Marie" together, although neither one wanted to, since the romantic lyrics said things they were not ready to admit in public.[14] They would also sing "Indian Love Call" at the local ice cream palace, where Chuck's friend Leo once cleverly informed them (and their impromptu audience) that romantic musical theater reached its height after the war with Romberg and Friml, citing Friml as the one "responsible for that love song of yours."[15]

Friml's legacy is much more than that of a musical emblem of nostalgia, for he contributed significantly and deeply to the development of the American musical theater. Like many midcentury Broadway musicals, those by Friml from the 1920s carried the moniker "musical play," demonstrating an intentional synthesis of song and story. He was also a master at using song to define character, something that would continue in the work of Rodgers and Hammerstein and their contemporaries, and was especially gifted in showing distinctions between various characters of the same gender, especially women, through music. For example, in *Rose Marie*, Rose Marie sings operetta, while Lady Jane intones musical comedy. And in *The Vagabond King*, Katherine's music is elegant and operatic whereas Huguette's is lyrical but certainly not operatic. These same distinctions reappear in shows such as *Oklahoma!*, where Laurie, who is extremely selective in her choice of men, is the progeny of Rose Marie and Katherine, and Ado Annie, who is "just a girl who cain't say no," follows in the steps of Lady Jane and Huguette.

Friml also advanced the musical theater in his ability to portray specific times and places through music. Authenticity was not paramount; this was theatrical entertainment, not documentary realism. Friml proved that established musical tropes could be effective in evoking specific ethnicities. The most obvious cases

Friml in the 1930s. Copyright Bettman / Corbis.

are the Native American elements in *Rose Marie* and *The White Eagle*. This musical creation of ethnicity is evident throughout the history of the Broadway musical in the second half of the twentieth century, including depictions of Highland Scots in *Brigadoon* (1947), Siamese royalty in *The King and I* (1951), Russian Jews in *Fiddler on the Roof* (1964), and Spaniards in *Man of La Mancha* (1965).

Friml's music was popular because it made people happy. The composer brought joy to millions through his music. On December 4, 1968, President Lyndon B. Johnson wrote him a birthday letter in which he paid homage to the composer:

> For decades, your musical composition has gladdened and uplifted the hearts of America— and, indeed, the world. It must be a source of continuing satisfaction to you to know the measure of joy that you have brought to so many.
>
> Please accept my warm admiration for your timeless contributions to the American heritage. It comes from a President who has always derived inspiration from the fierce, free spirit of the Czechoslovak people which, transplanted on our own shores, has so enriched us all.[16]

One year later, Ogden Nash wrote on the occasion of Friml's ninetieth birthday: "I trust that your conclusion and mine are similar: / T'would be a happier world if it were Frimler."[*17]

Friml believed in the cultivation of beauty, something he accomplished through music. In one of the most famous and beloved songs of his entire career, "Only a Rose," Friml and his librettist capture the splendor of a flower, likening it to human love. Just as Friml honored a flower, botanists privileged Friml by naming a hybrid variety of rhododendron after him. Like Friml's most famous songs, the plant is an evergreen. C. S. Seabrook developed the Rudolf Friml rhododendron in 1964. It is six feet tall with light green, medium-sized leaves. It has funnel-shaped solferino (purplish red) flowers that are three and a half inches wide grouped together in tight trusses.[18] The plant is sturdy and tall, like Friml's place in the American musical theater. Its flowers are of a particularly deep and vivid color, akin to the richness and lushness of Friml's finest music. Being a hybrid made it all the more appropriate, for Friml in his music did not just write in one style but rather chose the musical discourse that would best serve the needs of the individual situation and, in the case of a musical theater work, the inherent drama. The results were often striking.

---

* Copyright 1969 by Ogden Nash. Reprinted by permission of Curtis Brown, Ltd.

NOTES

CHAPTER 1: *From Prague to America*

1. Michael Chabon, *The Amazing Adventures of Kavalier & Clay* (New York: Picador USA, 2000).

2. "Rudolf Friml Dead in Hollywood at 92," *New York Times*, Nov. 14, 1972, 50.

3. Except where noted, material in this section comes from Friml's unpublished typescript autobiography. The work consists of chapters or essays ranging in length from one to twelve pages and is part of the Rudolf Friml Collection, 20, Music Library Special Collections, University of California, Los Angeles (hereafter "unpublished typescript").

4. Kay Friml, conversation with author, Los Angeles, June 8, 2004.

5. Of the multitude of Dvořák biographies, only Neil Butterworth's *Dvořák: His Life and Times* (New York: Hippocrene, 1984), 82, lists Friml among Dvořák's pupils.

6. Rudolf Friml, "Rudolf Friml Life Story: Notes, 'Anton Dvořák was a very busy man,'" unpublished typescript.

7. Tom Prideaux, "A Hymnl to Friml," *Life Magazine*, Jan. 23, 1970, R.

8. Jitřenka Pešková and Věra Nollová, letter to author, Mar. 30, 2004.

9. Friml, "Prague & the Conservatory," unpublished typescript.

10. Augustin Berger, "From the book 'Memoirs of Augustine [*sic*] Berger,'" unpublished typescript, Rudolf Friml Collection.

11. Ibid.

12. Ibid.

13. Josef Kotek, "Populárně poslechová (salónní) hudba před rokem 1918 a způsoby jejího uplatňování" [Czech Salon Music before 1918 and How It Made Its Way], *Hudební věda* [Musical Life] 28.3 (1991): 198, transl. David Kováč.

14. Vlasta Reittererová, "Skladatel měsíce: Rudolf Friml," *Harmonie* 11 (2002), http://www.muzikus.cz/klasicka-hudba-jazz-clanky/Skladatel-mesice-Rudolf-Friml~31~prosinec~2002/ (accessed June 19, 2007), transl. David Kováč.

15. Friml, "Rudolf Friml Life Story: Notes, 'I almost became an operatic composer,'" unpublished typescript.

16. Ibid.

17. Kotek, "Populárně poslechová," 199.

18. Berger, "From the book 'Memoirs of Augustine [*sic*] Berger.'"

19. Augustin Berger, with Ladislav Hájek, *Paměti Augustina Bergra* (Prague: Nakladatelství Orbis, 1942), 218, transl. David Kováč.

20. "Debut Statistics," typescript, Rudolf Friml Collection.

21. Josef Kotek, "Prvá setkání České hudby s jazzovými idiomy. K počátkům moderní populární hudby v Čechách" [The First Encounters of Czech Music with Jazz Idioms. Concerning the Origins of Modern Popular Music in Czechoslovakia], *Hudební věda* 9.4 (1992): 322, transl. David Kováč.

22. Ibid., 323.

23. Ibid.

24. Ibid., 322.

25. Henry Roth, *Violin Virtuosos: From Paganini to the 21st Century* (Los Angeles: California Classics Books, 1997), 65.

26. Jiří Dostál, *Jan Kubelík* (Prague: Školní Nakladateslství pro Čechy a Moravu, 1942), 33, transl. David Kováč.

27. Friml, "Rudolf Friml Life Story: Notes, 'When we were concertizing,'" unpublished typescript.

28. Roth, *Violin Virtuosos*, 61.

29. Appears as "Nocturno" in the printed program.

30. Program at the National Library of the Czech Republic, Prague.

31. From the report in the *Musical Courier* of Dec. 14, 1904, it is not clear which sonata Friml played. Rudolf Friml Collection.

32. Program listed in "Rudolf Friml Recital," *Musical Courier*, Dec. 14, 1904, Rudolf Friml Collection.

33. Friml, "Rudolf Friml Life Story: Notes, 'Carnegie Hall Debut,'" unpublished typescript.

34. The score to the concerto is in the Rudolf Friml Collection.

35. "Rudolf Friml's Debut," *Musical Courier*, Nov. 23, 1904, Rudolf Friml Collection.

36. "Two New Pianists," *New York Times*, Nov. 18, 1904, 6.

37. "Rudolf Friml's Debut."

38. *Rudolf Friml Piano Compositions: Educational Commentary and Catalogue* (New York: G. Schirmer, [1914]), 3–4.

39. Ibid., 41.

40. Anthony Tommasini, "Rudolf Friml, Beyond 'Indian Love Call,'" *New York Times*, July 18, 2004, AR-25.

CHAPTER 2: *The Emergence of a Broadway Composer*

1. Jeffrey Magee, "Ragtime and Early Jazz," in *The Cambridge History of American Music*, ed. David Nicholls (Cambridge: Cambridge University Press, 1998), 390.

2. Ibid.

3. For more on new dance styles on Broadway in the early twentieth century, see Agnes de Mille, *America Dances* (New York: Macmillan, 1980), especially chapter 7, "Popular Theater 1900–1930"; and Ian Driver, *A Century of Dance* (London: Octopus, 2000), especially chapter 2, "Ragtime Crazy," and chapter 3, "Running Wild."

4. Driver, *Century of Dance*, 28.

5. Ibid., 34–35.

6. For more on the construction of Ruritania, see Vesna Goldsworthy, *Inventing Ruritania: The Imperialism of the Imagination* (New Haven: Yale University Press, 1998); and Maria Todorova, *Imagining the Balkans* (New York: Oxford University Press, 1997).

7. Hugh Fordin, *Getting to Know Him: A Biography of Oscar Hammerstein II* (New York: Random House, 1977), 46.

8. "New Opera Made for Mlle. Trentini," *New York Times*, June 22, 1912, 13.

9. The production moved to the Casino Theatre on Dec. 30, 1912.

10. According to the playbill, the book was based on Leo Ditrichstein's farce *Before and After* (1905), itself an adaptation of the 1904 French farce *Les Dragées d'Hercule* (The Pills of Hercules).

11. Both songs were added after the show opened (Richard C. Norton, *A Chronology of American Musical Theater* [New York: Oxford University Press, 2002], 2:42).

12. "The Dixiana Rise" replaced an early song, "All Aboard for Dixie(land)," with music by George L. Cobb and lyrics by Jack Yellen.

13. "'High Jinks' Brings Good Cheer to Lyric," *New York Times*, Dec. 11, 1931, 11.

14. The script for *Katinka* in the Otto Harbach Papers at the New York Public Library gives alternative settings for acts 2 and 3: Old Anzali, Persia, for act 2, and the Café Parisienne in Paris for act 3.

15. Kurt Gänzl, *The British Musical Theatre* (New York: Oxford University Press, 1986), vol. 2, 31–32.

16. Edward W. Said, *Orientalism* (New York: Vintage Books, 1979).

17. See Rebecca A. Bryant, "Shaking Things Up: Popularizing the Shimmy in America," *American Music* 20.2 (2002): 168–87.

18. Rudolf Friml, "Rudolf Friml Life Story: Notes, 'In 1918, During World War I,'" unpublished typescript.

19. Kurt Gänzl, *The Encyclopedia of the Musical Theatre* (London: Blackwell, 1994), vol. 2, 1345.

20. For more on the cultivation of physical beauty at this time, see Lois W. Banner, *American Beauty* (New York: Knopf, 1983).

21. "Alice Nielsen in 'Kitty Darlin'," *New York Times*, Nov. 8, 1917, 13.

22. "Nancy Welford Stars in Tuneful 'Cinders'," *New York Times*, Apr. 4, 1923, 23.

23. Gerald Bordman, *American Musical Theatre: A Chronicle*, 3rd ed. (New York: Oxford University Press, 2001), 410.

24. Harry MacArthur, "Friml Music Is Very Much Alive," *Washington (D.C.) Evening Star*, June 29, 1965, A10.

CHAPTER 3: *Envisioning the West: 'Rose Marie'*

1. Ruth Ellen Gruber, "Deep in the Heart of Bavaria," *New York Times*, Apr. 11, 2004, TR6.

2. Lynn Dumenil, *The Modern Temper: American Culture and Society in the 1920s* (New York: Hill and Wang, 1995), 77.

3. Shari M. Huhndorf, *Going Native: Indians in the American Cultural Imagination* (Ithaca, N.Y.: Cornell University Press, 2001), 92.

4. For an analysis of *The Vanishing American* in light of Native American depictions, interpretation, and meanings, see Michael J. Riley, "Trapped in the History of Film: Racial Conflict and Allure in *The Vanishing American*," in *Hollywood's Indian: The Portrayal of the Native American in Film*, ed. Peter C. Rollins and John E. O'Connor (Lexington: University Press of Kentucky, 1998), 58–72.

5. Ibid., 67.

6. Jace Weaver, "Ethnic Cleansing, Homestyle," *Wicazo Sa Review* 10.1 (1994): 27.

7. The title of *Rose Marie* often appears in a hyphenated version: *Rose-Marie*. This applies to the title of the show and the song as well as to the name of the character. The published vocal score and Friml's own notes do not include the hyphen, though several playbills do. Technically, both titles are correct. For the sake of consistency, I will use the unhyphenated form when discussing the stage operetta.

8. Felicia Hardison Londré and Daniel J. Watermeier, *The History of North American Theater* (New York: Continuum, 2000), 183.

9. Hugh Fordin, *Getting to Know Him: A Biography of Oscar Hammerstein II* (New York: Random House, 1977), 54.

10. Rudolf Friml, "Herbert Stoddard [*sic*]," unpublished typescript.

11. Rudolf Friml, "Rudolf Friml Story: One Time during My Writing Operettas," unpublished typescript.

12. "Obituaries: Mary Ellis," *Opera News* 67.10 (2003): 79.

13. Deems Taylor, "Music: With Mary Ellis," *New York World*, Oct. 30, 1924.

14. Heywood Brown, untitled segment, *New York World*, Oct. 30, 1924; Alan Dale, "'Rose-Marie' Has Much of Merit at Imperial," *New York American*, Sept. 8, 1924.

15. Richard C. Norton, *A Chronology of American Musical Theater* (New York: Oxford University Press, 2002), 2:372.

16. See Michael V. Pisani, *Imagining Native America in Music* (New Haven: Yale University Press, 2005), and "'I'm an Indian Too': Creating Native American Identities in Nineteenth- and Early Twentieth-Century Music," in *The Exotic in Western Music*, ed. Jonathan Bellman (Boston: Northeastern University Press, 1998), 218–57.

17. Pisani, "'I'm an Indian Too,'" 229–30.

18. Weaver, "Ethnic Cleansing," 30.

19. Riley, "Trapped in the History of Film," 62.

20. Ibid., 67.

21. Fordin, *Getting to Know Him*, 58.

22. Ibid.

23. Ibid.

24. Ibid., 59.

25. Kurt Gänzl, *The Encyclopedia of the Musical Theatre* (London: Blackwell, 1994), vol. 2, 1240.

26. Ibid.

27. Lawrence J. Quirk, *The Films of Joan Crawford* (New York: Citadel Press, 1968), 56.

28. After the release of the 1954 film, this version was retitled *Indian Love Call* for television broadcast. The video release uses the original title.

29. Edward Baron Turk, *Hollywood Diva: A Biography of Jeanette MacDonald* (Berkeley: University of California Press, 1998), 173.

30. Ibid.

31. The Jorge Negrete version has been reissued on *Jorge Negrete: 40 Temas Originales* (RCA Victor 74321–72830–2). The *30 Inolvidables* recording was co-released by Univision Records and Warner Music Latina (issue number 0883 10156 2).

32. Bill C. Malone, *Country Music, U.S.A.*, 2nd ed. (Austin: University of Texas Press, 2002), 238.

33. The musical is based on the 1976 documentary film *Grey Gardens* by David Maysles, Albert Maysles, Ellen Hovde, Muffie Meyer, and Susan Froemke.

34. Dudley Do-Right was a recurring character on the *Rocky and Bullwinkle Show* and was the focus of the animated series *The Dudley Do-Right Show* in 1969.

35. For more on *Little Mary Sunshine*, see Raymond Knapp, *The American Musical and the Performance of Personal Identity* (Princeton, N.J.: Princeton University Press, 2006), 40–49.

36. "The Lumberjack Song" first appeared in season 1, episode 9, of *Monty Python's Flying Circus*, broadcast on the BBC on Dec. 14, 1969. Connie Booth played the "Lumberjack's Girl," and the Mountie chorus included Monty Python regulars and the Fred Tomlinson Singers. Terry Jones, Michael Palin, and Fred Tomlinson (who was also the arranger) composed the song to lyrics by Terry Jones and Michael Palin. In later versions on film, stage, and LP recording, the transition to the song was handled differently. Eric Idle sang the Lumberjack in some versions.

CHAPTER 4: *A Francophile Musical: 'The Vagabond King'*

1. Jean-Philippe Mathy, *French Resistance: The French-American Culture Wars* (Minneapolis: University of Minnesota Press, 2000), 34.

2. Alistair Horne, *Seven Ages of Paris* (New York: Knopf, 2003), 331.

3. Ibid.

4. Ibid.

5. Quoted in Patrice Higonnet, *Paris: Capital of the World* (Cambridge, Mass.: Belknap, 2002), 332.

6. Ibid., 325.

7. Ibid., 113.

8. Information on the creation of *The Vagabond King* comes from Rudolf Friml, "About an Operetta Named *The Vagabond King*," unpublished typescript.

9. The production transferred to the Century Theatre on Nov. 15, 1926.

10. Adelphi Theatre, Oct. 14, 1929; London Coliseum, Mar. 18, 1937, with Harry Welchman; and Winter Garden, Apr. 22, 1943.

11. C. B. D., "King Scores a Triumph in 'The Vagabond King'," *New York Herald-Tribune*, Sept. 22, 1925.

12. Stephen Rathbun, "'The Vagabond King' at Casino," *New York Sun*, Sept. 22, 1925.

13. Rudolf Friml, "Rudolf Friml Biography, 'After "Vagabond King" and "Rose Marie,"'" unpublished typescript.

14. David A. Fein, *François Villon Revisited* (New York: Twayne, 1997), 10, 13.

15. Ibid., 8, 9.

16. Ibid., 57.

17. Ibid., 169.

18. Friml, "About an Operetta Named *The Vagabond King.*"

19. Ibid.

20. Ibid.

21. Ibid.

22. For more on rose symbolism in the Middle Ages, see Sarah Carleton, "A Rose Is a Rose Is a Rose? The Rose as Symbol in the Ars Antiqua Motet," *Discourses in Music* 5.1 (Spring 2004), on-line journal available at www.discourses.ca/v5n1a1.html (accessed May 31, 2007).

23. Fein, *François Villon Revisited*, 2, 57.

24. "Rudolf Friml Returns from Concert Tour," *Los Angeles Times*, May 11, 1966.

25. Rudolf Friml to Lyndon B. Johnson, typed letter, Dec. 9, 1968, Rudolf Friml Collection.

26. Edward Baron Turk, *Hollywood Diva: A Biography of Jeanette MacDonald* (Berkeley: University of California Press, 1998), 93.

27. The trio also wrote "King Louie" and "Mary, Queen of Heaven" for the film, while only Robin and Chase wrote "What France Needs" and "Death March."

28. Huguette's "Love for Sale" was cut from the film. Lillian Roth, who played Huguette, had nearly as much screen time as MacDonald. Edward Baron Turk wrote that her singing style in "Huguette's Waltz" was akin to "Lotte Lenya with a Brooklyn accent" (Turk, *Hollywood Diva*, 92).

29. Turk, *Hollywood Diva*, 90.

30. Ibid., 91.

31. Ibid., 91–92.

CHAPTER 5: *The Challenge of Success*

1. Hugh Fordin, *Getting to Know Him: A Biography of Oscar Hammerstein II* (New York: Random House, 1977), 64.

2. For more on Romberg's operettas, see William A. Everett, *Sigmund Romberg*, Yale Broadway Masters (New Haven: Yale University Press, 2007). Chapters 4–6 focus on Romberg's work from the 1920s.

3. Quoted in Gene Lees, "In Love with Life," *High Fidelity* 22.11 (1972): 19.

4. Fordin, *Getting to Know Him*, 66.

5. J. Brooks Atkinson, "'The White Eagle' Is Lavishly Staged," *New York Times*, Dec. 27, 1927, 24.

6. According to Friml, "Give Me One Hour" was composed for tenor Richard Tauber, who was ill at the time. "Give me one hour," whispered Tauber to the composer, "and I will try to sing for you." Friml wrote the song while Tauber was convalescing (liner notes for *Rudolf Friml Plays His Own Unforgettable Melodies*, Decca DL 5389). Friml fails to address how he obtained Hooker's lyrics for the song.

7. J. Brooks Atkinson, "'All for One,'" *New York Times*, Mar. 25, 1928, sec. 9, 1.

8. J. Brooks Atkinson, "The Play: 'The Three Musketeers,'" *New York Times*, Mar. 14, 1928, 28.

9. Atkinson, "'All for One.'"

10. The waltz replaced a duple-meter ballad, "Heart of Mine," after the show opened (Richard C. Norton, *A Chronology of American Musical Theater* [New York: Oxford University Press, 2002], 2:31).

11. Untitled article, *New York Times*, Sept. 18, 1930, 28.

12. "Hammerstein Ends 'Luana' Run Tonight," *New York Times*, Oct. 4, 1930, 15.

13. John Shubert was the son of impresario J. J. Shubert.

14. Brooks McNamara, *The Shuberts of Broadway* (New York: Oxford University Press, 1990), 159.

15. Maria Jeritza (1887–1982) was a famous Czech soprano who sang at the Metropolitan Opera from 1921 to 1932. She created the role of Ariadne in *Ariadne auf Naxos* (1912) and was the first empress in *Die Frau ohne Schatten* (1918). She was especially known for her *verismo* roles, including Tosca, Minnie, Turandot (all Puccini) and Jenůfa (Janáček).

16. Gilbert W. Gabriel, "'Music Hath Charms': The Messrs. Shubert Go to Venice with a Friml Score," *New York American*, Dec. 31, 1935; [J.] Brooks Atkinson, "The Play: Conventional Operetta in 'Music Hath Charms,' with a Score by Rudolf Friml," *New York Times*, Dec. 31, 1934, 8.

CHAPTER 6: *Away from Broadway*

1. Edward Baron Turk, *Hollywood Diva: A Biography of Jeanette MacDonald* (Berkeley: University of California Press, 1998), 96.

2. Edwin M. Bradley, *The First Hollywood Musicals: A Critical Filmography of 171 Features, 1927 through 1932* (Jefferson, N.C.: McFarland, 1996), 203.

3. Turk, *Hollywood Diva*, 213.

4. Ibid., 214–15.

5. Ibid., 214.

6. Ibid.

7. "Favorite Melodies Old and New," in souvenir book for the film version of *The Firefly*, n.d., 7, Rudolf Friml Collection.

8. Ibid.

9. "'Firefly' Flashes," in souvenir book for the film version of *The Firefly*, 16, author's personal collection.

10. Turk, *Hollywood Diva*, 215.

11. Edward Heyman was the lyricist and Herbert J. Yates was the producer. Elizabeth Meehan and Richard Sale based the screenplay on an original story by Angela Stuart.

12. "Rudolf Friml, 69, Rides Bike to Beach for Swim," *Los Angeles Times*, Dec. 8, 1953, Rudolf Friml file, Margaret Herrick Library.

13. Evelyn De Wolfe, "She Walks All Over Rudolf Friml, 90," *Los Angeles Times*, Sept. 25, 1970, Rudolf Friml file, Margaret Herrick Library.

14. Ibid.

15. Mrs. Rudolf Friml to Dr. Pechold, no date indicated, Kay Friml notes, Rudolf Friml Collection.

16. "Nothing Left to Steal, Insists Mlle. Trentini," unidentified newspaper clipping, Center for American History, University of Texas at Austin.

17. "Friml Becomes a Citizen," unidentified newspaper clipping, Center for American History, University of Texas at Austin.

18. Material in this paragraph comes from Kay Friml's handwritten notes in the Rudolf Friml Collection.

19. Kay Friml notes, Rudolf Friml Collection.

20. "Friml Finishes Biog," *Hollywood Reporter*, Jan. 11, 1957. Rudolf Friml (-1959) file, Margaret Herrick Library.

21. Ibid.

22. These are in the form of short chapters ranging in length from one to twelve pages. Many chapters contain retellings of events related in other chapters. The typescript is in the Rudolf Friml Collection.

23. "Rudolf Friml (1879–1972)," unpublished typescript, Rudolf Friml Collection.

24. Milton Berliner, "Rudolf Friml, at 85, Keeps Himself in Tune," *Washington Daily News*, June 29, 1965, 14.

25. Rudolf Friml, *How I Keep My Technique: Melodic Studies for Piano*, 3 vols. (New York: Robbins Music Corporation, 1950). These books are out of print in 2007.

26. These tapes are now in the Rudolf Friml Collection.

27. Kay Friml, conversation with author, Los Angeles, June 8, 2004.

28. Bob Thomas, "Friml Starts New Career," *Los Angeles Herald Examiner*, June 6, 1962, Rudolf Friml file, Margaret Herrick Library.

29. Milton Berliner, "Friml Was in No Hurry," *Washington Daily News*, June 29, 1965, 14.

30. Paul Hume, "Friml Reminisces at Keyboard Here," *Washington Post*, June 29, 1965, C12.

31. Doris Reno, "Friml's 'Dash, Versatility' Delight Overflow Audiences," *Miami Herald*, n.d., presumably 1966, Rudolf Friml Collection.

32. Kay Friml, conversation with author, Los Angeles, June 8, 2004.

33. Reno, "Friml's 'Dash, Versatility' Delight Overflow Audiences."

34. Jo Werne, "Composer Friml, 87: 1,500 Toss a Party," *Miami Herald*, Dec. 8, 1966, 14–C.

35. Unpublished scripts for both programs are in the Rudolf Friml Collection.

36. Elise K. Kirk, *Music at the White House: A History of the American Spirit*, Music in American Life (Urbana: University of Illinois Press, 1986), 288.

37. Thomas Buckley, "Friml Writes First Lady a Song and His Last Choice Records It," *New York Times*, July 28, 1963, 66.

38. All the works in this section are unpublished; many scores and parts are in the Rudolf Friml Collection.

39. "A Centenary Tribute: Rudolf Friml, King of Melody," *Opera Canada* 20.4 (1979): 11; Kay Friml notes, Rudolf Friml Collection.

40. Kay Friml notes, Rudolf Friml Collection.

41. Ibid.

42. "Friml—the Epitome of the 'Pops': He Returns for Concert," *San Francisco Examiner*, Aug. 16, 1962, 29.

43. The alternate titles *Czechoslovakian Rhapsody* and *Czech Rural Fantasy* appear on some orchestral parts.

44. The three movements are I. Allegro moderato, II. Espressivo, and III. Molto allegro. Nick Bolin arranged the orchestral parts, including parts for violin A, B, C, and D. The score for the second and third movements and parts for all three movements are in the Rudolf Friml Collection. Albert Glasser orchestrated the work, dating the second movement June 5, 1961, and the third June 10, 1961.

45. Arranged by Joseph Nussbaum, June 1956.

46. Albert Glasser transcribed and orchestrated the six-minute work, completing it on July 4, 1967.

47. Orchestrated by Albert Glasser, Dec. 1, 1961.

48. Walter Hinckle, "New Friml Enraptures the Pops," *San Francisco Chronicle*, Aug. 16, 1962, 41.

49. Orchestrated by Albert Glasser, Dec. 9, 1962.

50. Uncredited liner notes, *The Classical Friml*, Friml Phonograph Co. S-7777 (LP).

51. Arranged and orchestrated by Albert Glasser, Oct. 18, 1965.

52. Arranged by E. Zeisel and originally titled *Misty Morning*. *Misty Morning* is marked out on several orchestral parts, likely to distinguish it from another work with the same title.

53. Arranged by Nick Bolin.

54. Arranged by Albert Glasser.

55. Arranged by Stephan Pasternacki.

56. *The Stone Is Rolled Away* has words by J. Keirn Brennan and was published in *G. Schirmer's Editions of Oratorios and Cantatas*, Ed. 1766 (1943).

57. Liner notes for *Spirit of America*, unpublished typescript, Rudolf Friml Collection. Albert Glasser orchestrated the work, signing the score at the end "Brentwood, May 12, 1963."

58. Mrs. Rudolf Friml to Dr. Pechold, undated letter.

CHAPTER 7: *Reputation and Legacy*

1. Rudolf Friml, "About an Operetta Named *The Vagabond King*," unpublished typescript.

2. "The Three Musketeers," *Variety* 317, Nov. 14, 1984, 100.

3. Brendan Gill, "Grave Robbers," *New Yorker* 60, Nov. 19, 1984, 184.

4. Erika Munk, "Swashbungled," *Village Voice* 29, Nov. 20, 1984, 113.

5. "The Three Musketeers."

6. Gill, "Grave Robbers."

7. Vernon Scott, "Rudolph Friml, 90, at Piano 6 Hours a Day," UPI article, *Troy (N.Y.) Record*, Dec. 11, 1969, Rudolf Friml Collection.

8. Bob Thomas, "Friml Starts New Career," *Los Angeles Herald Examiner*, June 6, 1962, Rudolf Friml file, Margaret Herrick Library.

9. Ibid.

10. Gene Lees, "In Love with Life," *High Fidelity* 22.11 (1972): 19.

11. "Rudolf Friml Flays Musicals of Today," *Los Angeles Times*, Sept. 11, 1958, Rudolf Friml file, Margaret Herrick Library.

12. Scott, "Rudolf Friml, 90, at Piano 6 Hours a Day," "Composer Friml: Music's

Future: Not Melodious," *Boca Raton News,* Dec. 14, 1969, "Friml Condemns Today's Music," *Pittsburgh Press,* Dec. 28, 1969, and elsewhere, Rudolf Friml Collection.

13. Andrew M. Greeley, *A Christmas Wedding* (New York: Tom Doherty Associates, 2000).

14. Ibid., 35.

15. Ibid., 36.

16. Lyndon B. Johnson to Rudolf Friml, typed letter signed, Dec. 4, 1968, Rudolf Friml Collection.

17. Quoted in "Rudolf Friml Dead in Hollywood at 92," *New York Times,* Nov. 14, 1972, 50.

18. Homer E. Salley and Harold E. Greer, *Rhododendron Hybrids: A Guide to Their Origins* (Portland, Ore.: Timber Press, 1986), 284.

SELECTED WORKS

Operettas and Musical Comedies (Complete Scores)

The following list includes the lyricist/librettist, location and date of the Broadway premiere, and the number of performances.

The Firefly, Otto Hauerbach, Lyric Theatre, Dec. 2, 1912 (120).

High Jinks, Otto Hauerbach, Lyric Theatre, Dec. 10, 1913, moved to the Casino Theatre on Jan. 12, 1914 (213).

Katinka, Otto Hauerbach, 44th Street Theatre, Dec. 22, 1915 (220).

You're in Love, Otto Hauerbach and Edward Clark, Casino Theatre, Feb. 6, 1917 (167).

Kitty Darlin', Otto Hauerbach and P. G. Wodehouse, Casino Theatre, Nov. 7, 1917 (14).

Sometime, Rida Johnson Young, Shubert Theatre, Oct. 14, 1918 (283).

Glorianna, Catherine Chisholm Cushing, Liberty Theatre, Oct. 28, 1918 (96).

Tumble In, Otto Hauerbach, Selwyn Theatre, Mar. 24, 1919 (128).

The Little Whopper, Bide Dudley and Otto Harbach/Otto Harbach, Casino Theatre, Oct. 13, 1919 (204).

June Love, Brian Hooker/Otto Harbach and W. H. Post, Knickerbocker Theatre, Apr. 25, 1921 (48).

The Blue Kitten, Otto Harbach and William Carey Duncan, Selwyn Theatre, Jan. 13, 1922, moved to the East Carroll Theatre on May 1, 1922 (140).

Cinders, Edward Clark, Dresden Theatre, Apr. 3, 1923 (31).

Rose Marie, Otto Harbach and Oscar Hammerstein 2nd, Imperial Theatre, Sept. 2, 1924 (557).

The Vagabond King, Brian Hooker and W. H. Post, Casino Theatre, Sept. 21, 1925, moved to the Century Theatre on Nov. 15, 1926 (511).

The Wild Rose, Otto Harbach, Martin Beck Theatre, Oct. 20, 1926 (61).

The White Eagle, Brian Hooker and W. H. Post, Casino Theatre, Dec. 26, 1927 (48).

The Three Musketeers, William Anthony McGuire/Clifford Grey and P. G. Wodehouse, Lyric Theatre, Mar. 13, 1928 (319).

Luana, J. Keirn Brennan/Howard Emmett Rogers, Hammerstein's Theatre, Sept. 17, 1930 (21).

Music Hath Charms, Rowland Leigh, George Rosener, and John Shubert, Majestic Theatre, Dec. 29, 1934 (25).

Musical Theater Productions
(Individual Songs and Interpolations)

The Peasant Girl (1914)
Ziegfeld Follies of 1921 (1921)
Ziegfeld Follies of 1923 (1923)
Dew Drop Inn (1923)
In Love with Love (1923)
Annie Dear (1924)
Ziegfeld's Palm Beach Girl (1926)
Ruth Selwyn's 9:15 Revue (1930)
Rose Marie (additional songs, 1950)

Film Musicals

The Lottery Bride (1930, lyrics by J. Keirn Brennan)
Northwest Outpost (1947, lyrics by Edward Heyman)

Films (Incidental Music and Songs)

Rose-Marie (1936, additional songs, lyrics by Gus Kahn)
Music for Madame (1937, lyrics by Gus Kahn)
The Firefly (1937, additional songs, lyrics by Gus Kahn,
    Chet Forrest, and Bob Wright)
Katakomby [Catacombs] (1940)
Za Tichých Nocí [Through Quiet Nights] (1941)
Rose Marie (1954, additional songs, lyrics by Paul F. Webster)
The Vagabond King (1956, additional songs, lyrics by Johnny Burke)

Solo Piano Works

Spirit of the Woods (1905)
Aubade, op. 25 (1907)
Mignonette, op. 26 (1907)
Bohemian Dance, op. 29 (1907)
Staccato Etude, op. 37 (1908)
Grand Concert Mazurka, op. 40 (1908)
Egyptian Dance, op. 41 (1908)
Humoresque, op. 45 (1908)
California Suite, op. 57 (1910)
Mazurka, op. 68 (1910)
Butterfly Dance, op. 77, no. 1 (1911)
Valse Lucille, op. 85, no. 1 (1916)
Intermezzo, op. 85, no. 2 (1916)
Iris (1918)

Woodland Echoes (1918)
From My Garden (1918)
Russian Rural Scene (1919)
Chanson (1920)
Po Ling and Ming Toy: A Chinese Suite (1924)
"So You Are—Trés charmant" (1963)

Song Cycles

Písné Závišovy [Songs of Záviš], op. 1 (1901, texts by Jan Červenka)
Nové písně Závišovy [New Songs of Záviš], op. 14 (1905, texts by Jan Červenka)
Na struně lásky [On the String of Love], op. 19 (1909, texts by Karl Hašler)

Songs

"L'amour, toujours, l'amour" (1922, lyrics by Catherine Chisolm Cushing)
"The Lost World" (1924, lyrics by Harry B. Smith)
"Jacqueline" (1963, lyrics by Forman Brown, to piano piece "So You Are—
    Trés charmant")

Chamber Music

Piano Trio (Czech Rural Life), op. 36 (publ. 1918)

Orchestral Music

"Slavnost Chrysanthem" [Festival of the Chrysanthemums] (1899)
Piano Concerto in B-flat major, op. 10 (1904)
Auf Japan [From Japan] (1905)
Indiánská piseň [Indian Song] (1905)
Happy Days in Prater (1959)
Exodus to Hong Kong (1961)
Bohemian Club Concerto (1961)
Czech Rhapsody (1962)
Matterhorn (1962)
Scherzo-Tarantella (1962)
Slavonic Rhapsody (1962)
Scenes from My Youth (1962)
The Bells of Rome (1963)

Choral Music

The Stone Is Rolled Away (1943)
"Don't Take My Jesus Away" (1950)
Spirit of America (1963)

FOR FURTHER READING

Banfield, Stephen. "Popular Song and Popular Music on Stage and Film." In *The Cambridge History of American Music*, ed. David Nicholls. Cambridge: Cambridge University Press, 1998. 309–44.

Bordman, Gerald. *American Musical Theatre: A Chronicle*. 3rd ed. New York: Oxford University Press, 2001.

———. *American Operetta*. New York: Oxford University Press, 1981.

Everett, William A. "American and British Operetta in the 1920s: Romance, Nostalgia and Adventure." In *The Cambridge Companion to the Musical*, 2nd ed., ed. William A. Everett and Paul R. Laird. Cambridge: Cambridge University Press, 2008. 72–88.

Gänzl, Kurt. *The Musical: A Concise History*. Boston: Northeastern University Press, 1997.

Green, Stanley. *The World of Musical Comedy*. 4th ed. San Diego: A. S. Barnes, 1980; reprint ed., New York: Da Capo, 1984.

Lamb, Andrew. *150 Years of Popular Musical Theatre*. New Haven: Yale University Press, 2000.

Mordden, Ethan. *Make Believe: The Broadway Musical in the 1920s*. New York: Oxford University Press, 1997.

Traubner, Richard. *Operetta: A Theatrical History*. Garden City, N.Y.: Doubleday, 1983; 2nd ed., Lanham, Md.: Scarecrow, 2004.

SUGGESTED LISTENING

Individual Shows

The Firefly. Ohio Light Opera, Jason Altieri, conductor. Recorded in 2006. Albany TROY 891–92. 2 CDs.

Rose Marie. Highlights. Linden Singers, New World Show Orchestra, Johnny Douglas, Rita Williams Singers, Tony Osborne & His Orchestra. Recorded in 1957 and 1961. EMI Classics for Pleasure 0946 3 35971 2 9 (with *The Vagabond King* highlights).

Rose-Marie. 1999 Media Theatre Cast Recording. Media Theatre IND99222.

The Vagabond King. Selections. Alfred Drake, Mimi Benzell, Frances Bible, Orchestra and Chorus under the direction of Jay Blackton. Recorded in 1951. Decca 440 018 731–2 (with *Roberta*).

The Vagabond King. Selections. John Hanson, Jane Fyfee, The Peter Knight Orchestra and Chorus. Recorded in 1960. Castle Communications MAC CD 334 (with *The Student Prince*).

The Vagabond King. Highlights. Peter Knight Singers, New World Show Orchestra, Jan Červenka. Recorded in 1961. EMI Classics for Pleasure 0946 3 35971 2 9 (with *Rose Marie* highlights).

The Vagabond King. Ohio Light Opera, Steven Byess, conductor. Recorded in 2004. Albany TROY 738–39. 2 CDs.

Collections

Bygone Days: Music for Violin and Piano by Rudolf Friml. Stephanie Chase, violin, Sara Davis Buechner, piano. Koch Classics KIC-CD-7662 (2006).

Friml Plays Friml. Rudolf Friml, piano, Ivo Zidek, tenor. Recorded in Prague, Sept. 28, 1964. Supraphon SU 3267–2 911 (1996 CD reissue).

Piano Music of Rudolf Friml. Sara Davis Buechner. Koch Classics 3-7512-2 HI (2003).

The Romantic World of Rudolf Friml. Various artists. Flapper PAST CD 9764 (n.d.).

Rudolf Friml: Chansonette. Eastman-Dryden Orchestra, Donald Hunsberger, conductor, Teresa Ringholz, soprano. Arabesque Z6562 (1986).

INDEX

Composers

Lou Harrison
*Leta E. Miller and
Fredric Lieberman*
John Cage
David Nicholls
Dudley Buck
N. Lee Orr
William Grant Smith
Catherine Parsons Smith
Rudolf Friml
William Everett

WILLIAM EVERETT is associate professor and area coordinator of musicology at the University of Missouri–Kansas City Conservatory of Music and Dance. His research areas include American musical theater and the creation of place and national identity in music. His books include *Sigmund Romberg, The Musical: A Research and Information Guide, On Bunker's Hill: Essays in Honor of J. Bunker Clark* (coeditor), *Historical Dictionary of the Broadway Musical* (coauthor), and *The Cambridge Companion to the Musical* (coeditor).

The University of Illinois Press
is a founding member of the
Association of American University Presses.

Composed in 9.5/13 Janson Text
with Meta and Janson display
by Celia Shapland
at the University of Illinois Press
Designed by Copenhaver Cumpston
Manufactured by Thomson-Shore, Inc.

UNIVERSITY OF ILLINOIS PRESS

1325 South Oak Street Champaign, IL 61820-6903
www.press.uillinois.edu